COACHING
WITH
VALUES

"This is an important book that brings values back into the heart of coaching. What I loved about this book is the rich map and guide Lindsay presents that coaches and clients can use to align values with life and career direction. Lindsay's experience and expertise lends itself to a refreshing and insightful read with great questions and techniques. This is the book I needed when I started coach training and one I will be using to ensure I stay on track."

Jackee Holder
Leadership Coach, Author and Speaker
www.jackeeholder.com

"The training I received from Values Coach UK has proved to be invaluable in helping me to develop my own values coaching business. Lindsay's approach is highly professional, totally committed and very stimulating. Her training courses and workshops delivered exactly what she promised and ensured that her exhaustive understanding of the subject was passed on to each and every delegate. It has been a pleasure for me to take the learning, develop it in my business and see my clients benefit."

Rowena Wild
Values Coach

"Lindsay's values process and tools gave me the vocabulary to describe what I had personally been sensing and experiencing for a long time. Her techniques can be used on self, individuals and teams both in the workplace and at home. My clients love the structured values elicitation process which helps them to bring focus to dilemmas and clarity to decisions. Not so much of a text book but a good read and presentation of 'eureka' moments, deciphering why we react in certain ways in different situations. Would highly recommend to all!"

Maia Rushby
Values Coach & Consultant

"Lindsay West's coaching is awesome. What an insight into myself, my values, my beliefs, my perceptions and most importantly my expectations based on those things! Let me say that if you really want to know who you are and what you stand for, have a session... it is a revelation! At last I know that 'making a difference' is right at my core! Magnificent."

Jenni Russell, Author, CHEK Practitioner and Holistic Lifestyle Coach (Level 1)

"Now that I understand my values it is clear to me what is really important in my life. By honouring my core values I know this will increase my satisfaction.
When it comes to making decisions a check in with my values reaffirms the choices I've made and ensures I'm going in the right direction.
I can recognise why I feel the way I do about something if it compromises my values."

Mr. J Connolly, Producer

COACHING
WITH
VALUES

How to put values at the heart of your coaching
to make a lasting difference.

LINDSAY WEST

AuthorHouse™ UK
1663 Liberty Drive
Bloomington, IN 47403 USA
www.authorhouse.co.uk
Phone: 0800.197.4150

Published by AuthorHouse 06/24/2015

ISBN: 978-1-5049-3918-8 (sc)
ISBN: 978-1-5049-3919-5 (e)

for Mike

for supporting me in living my values every day

Contents

Part 1: About Values

The first part of 'Coaching with Values' introduces values, explains in detail what they are and what they are not. It then shows where our values come from and how we form them. It covers how and when they may change in our lives and it explains why values are important to us in life and as coaches.

Part 2: The I-VALUE Coaching Framework

The second part of 'Coaching with Values' details the I-VALUE Coaching methodology, which incorporates a coaching framework, the process and a detailed set of techniques for each stage. It includes examples and case studies.

Introduction

Welcome to 'Coaching with Values', the first in a series of books about how to put values at the heart of your coaching to make a bigger and lasting difference to those you coach.

Let me start by asking you two questions...

Do you want to be happier, healthier and more successful?

Do you want to make a bigger difference in the world and increase your income doing so?

If the answer is yes to one or both of these questions, you can make it happen and you are reading the right book to help you. So relax, read on and enjoy.

Perhaps, in your coaching practice, you are not quite where you want to be. You are following your passion but don't have enough income. It could be that you work really hard but are not getting the results you want. Maybe you spend too much time working and do not have enough time for family and friends. If you coach people as part of your employed role, perhaps you are unsure if you are really making a difference to them.

Has this gone on long enough, are you ready to make a change?

You could be reading this book to learn new skills and become even better as a coach. Imagine if you had more clients, you would be making a difference to more people and earning more money doing exactly what you love. Wouldn't it be great if you were successful enough to do all those things you dream about...taking more holidays, going on more courses or perhaps investing more in your business?

As coaches our purpose is to take people from where they are now to where they want to be. My purpose is to take your business or career from where it is now to where you want it to be.

Coaching has been around for a good while now but perhaps too often is about fixing problems, rather than preventing them in the first place.

In this book you will discover how understanding and living your values means you do what is important to you. By making the right decisions and choices in life for you, you can avoid problems and don't lose time following the wrong path. The benefits of using values in this way are long lasting and can make a big difference to your future and that of those you coach.

I believe that as a society, we have moved away from our values, becoming too focused on material things, judging others and comparing ourselves to others. We have lost sight of what is truly important to us.

> *Have you ever felt you are living your life for others but at a cost to yourself?*

Ten years ago I decided to stop making choices that served others at a huge expense to myself. I started to serve others in a way that has given me great happiness, success and significantly better health.

I'd had a good career in banking and had fully immersed myself in the 'work-hard, play hard' culture. I had spent many years working really long hours, travelling up and down the country, studying in every free minute and rarely seeing my partner. I'd been eating food on the go, not getting enough sleep, drinking too much and getting no exercise.

Until one day, when I was told that I had a new boss, who expected my loyalty and respect, even though I had more experience and better qualifications than him. I hadn't been given the opportunity to apply for the role and this was the third time it had happened.

My health was suffering, my marriage was over, my career had hit that infamous 'glass ceiling'. I passed the MBA but couldn't apply what I learned in the job I was doing. What was the point of it all? So I decided,

> '*Today is the day I start living my life for me and stop living it for them.*'

The next year I divorced, took redundancy, sold my house and gave myself a new beginning.

I had always loved developing my team and I had found a new interest in Neuro Linguistic Programming (NLP) whilst studying for the MBA. I trained as a coach and Master NLP Practitioner. It was during this training that I came to understand what values are and why they are important.

The world of finance I had left was full of espoused and expected values and very little behaviour that actually honoured those values. I started to understand which values really mattered to me and rebuilt my life and career around them.

I met someone new and we started a family together. I set up my own coaching and training business and put values at the heart of everything I do. I am now happier, healthier and more successful than I have ever been.

I have used a values-based approach in my coaching practice for over ten years and have found it to be fundamental in helping those I coach to find and sustain happiness and success in their lives.

My vision is to make an even bigger difference, by sharing this approach with coaches across the world. Through this book and through Values Coach training, I aim to enable both coaches and those they coach to understand the importance of values and to start living their values every day.

Most coaches see their role as supporting or facilitating others in achieving success, fulfilment and happiness in their lives and careers.

There are three key challenges in achieving this:

1. understanding what makes people feel happy and fulfilled;

2. helping people to make the changes needed in their lives to attain those feelings;

3. giving them the tools to sustain those changes and attain those feelings for the rest of their lives.

Over the last decade, I have worked with hundreds of personal clients and many organisations and have found that the single most effective way of addressing these three challenges is through values.

I have combined values with standard coaching techniques, with NLP techniques and many others to develop the 'I-VALUE Coaching' methodology.

'Coaching with Values' details the methodology. It includes the framework, processes, values-based techniques, examples and case studies. It is designed to teach those already practising coaching to use a values-based approach and help those they coach to live a values-led life.

Part 1 of Coaching with Values introduces Values, explains what they are, where they come from, why they are important in our lives and in coaching.

Part 2 details the 'I-VALUE Coaching' methodology, providing a comprehensive framework and set of techniques.

The methodology starts by exploring the issues faced and identifying core values then progresses to raising awareness of the changes needed.

It provides techniques to help people to live a values-led life by using values for many aspects that people find challenging: goal-setting, managing emotions (including enhancing motivation, increasing confidence and reducing stress) and making change (including decision-making, problem-solving and action planning).

Understanding the values of others, and the importance of this in communication, is also addressed.

The methodology has been developed into the Values Coach training programme, which provides qualified coaches with the opportunity to learn and practise the values-based techniques. Details are available on the www.valuescoach.co.uk website.

Whilst this book is primarily written for coaches, the approach and techniques are appropriate for all those using coaching skills; managers and leaders in organisations, trainers, teachers, counsellors, psychotherapists, complementary therapists.

Background Context

It seems more and more people are turning to coaching. Some are unhappy and dissatisfied with their lives and careers; some have achieved their goals and are left wondering what to do next; others have had change forced upon them. Whatever the reason, there is a thirst for answers to questions about what makes people feel happy and fulfilled and how they can sustain that feeling.

In a world where global organisations, governments and the media are now being held to account for the disastrous consequences of their poor behaviour and bad decision-making, we seek a way to rebuild our economy, our country, our society and in many cases our lives.

Those in positions of power had perhaps lost sight of what many of us deem to be important and the focus has now shifted to find a way to get us back on the right track.

Politicians, corporate executives and media leaders cannot make this happen alone. We each play a part in transforming the world we live in, to a world we want to live in, where we can all thrive, not just survive.

My experience in the corporate world, in business and especially as a coach have shown me that living and working by a core set of values is as essential to every individual as it is to every organisation.

Making decisions, choosing behaviour as well as language and taking actions that honour those core values is as crucial to creating lasting individual happiness and fulfilment as it is to sustainable business success.

Part 1:

About Values

1. What are Values?

Most people have an idea of what values are. Most know they are important, but few know which values are most important to them. Values influence people's behaviour and emotions every day, but few people use them as a positive guide to the way they live their lives. There are hundreds of values. There are some we all share. It is the combination of values that we hold that contributes to our uniqueness.

Values are the things that are important to us, the foundation of our lives. They are deeply held principles that guide our choices and behaviours and influence our emotions.

Values are the core of who we are. They are the fundamental things that need to be present in our lives for us to feel happiness, satisfaction and fulfilment. They are our motivators, the things that 'make us tick', the passion in our hearts and the reason why we do the things we do.

Values provide us with the unconscious 'why' for all of our actions and choices; they are the reason we do the things we do. They are often single words or short phrases that stand for abstract concepts we are expressing in our lives.

Some examples of values are:

• Making a difference	• Honesty
• Contribution	• Trust
• Success	• Love
• Achievement	• Loyalty
• Wellbeing	• Independence
• Security	• Support
• Protection	• Kindness
• Freedom	• Service
• Sense of belonging	• Collaboration

A fuller set of values is listed in Part 2, under 'Values Exploration'.

Of the many different values, each has a certain degree of importance to us, individually. The key to using values is to understand which values are *most* important to us.

When I talk about **core values**, I mean our Top 10 most important ones, in prioritised order. This prioritised set of core values makes us who we are and gives us our uniqueness. They are the ones that need to be present and need to be honoured in our lives, for us to feel happy and fulfilled.

The technique for exploring and identifying core values is covered in Part 2, under 'Values Exploration'.

I am often asked if our values change. I believe that our values do not change, they will always be important to us. However, what does change is the prioritisation of our values, in their relation to each other.

Circumstances, experiences, influences in our lives cause the prioritisation of our values to change. Major life events like marriage, child-birth, divorce, redundancy, bereavement have an influence on our values. As a result, certain values become more important to us at that point in our lives, than others.

This is covered in more detail in the next Chapter.

Values that are important to most people are ones such as security and love, which are fundamental to human beings. However, interestingly, when people have always felt loved and secure, these values can be taken for granted and may not feature in their Top 10 core values.

If someone does not feel secure and loved or these things have been taken away, then it is likely that these two values will feel important; however the prioritisation of these two values is affected by recent experience in a different way. Redundancy can rock people's sense of security, so a recent experience of this tends to cause people to value security much more highly. Whereas the break-up of a recent relationship can often leave people bitter and love is the last value they want to prioritise in their lives.

Sometimes, in order to identify a value we hold, we can explore a negative emotion to find the value that is missing, or not being honoured in a situation. One of the values that we often discover in ourselves in this way is the value of fairness. It is only when someone is being unfair to us or when we witness an injustice that we realise how important fairness is to us.

It is crucial for us to find exactly the right word to describe the value that is important. Values such as honesty, openness, trust and integrity are quite similar, so the key is to decide which word resonates most and is most meaningful for us, when identifying our core values.

I have found that sometimes the word we use to describe a value changes as we mature. This may be due to life experience or an increased understanding of what is important to us.

For example, a value of achievement may be extremely important to us and a big motivator in our twenties and thirties, then later in life, with maturity perhaps, the word success better describes the value we hold. Another example would be honesty, which may describe the value we feel is important to us in our youth. However, with maturity, for some, this may expand into a value of integrity.

Another observation I have made is that when people are asked what is important to them, they often respond with words like family, health or money; for me these are not values, these are 'chunk' words or collective nouns and are pitched at too generic a level to be meaningful as values.

As part of the process of understanding our values, we need to look a little deeper into ourselves at what these things give us, only then do we get closer to finding our core values. For example: from family we might get a sense of love, support or kindness, these are the true values. From having good health, we might get a sense of wellbeing or vitality. Money might give us security, choice or freedom.

We will hold different values in different aspects of our lives, for example in terms of career we might value responsibility, recognition and sense of achievement; whereas, in our home life, we might have values of stability, happiness and love.

In our relationships with friends, we might value fun, honesty and loyalty. In interests or hobbies, things like excitement, growth and contribution might be important to us. There may also be some cross-over, so values like fairness and respect may be important to us in all aspects of our lives and in all our relationships.

There are many values that we feel are important to us and important to see in those around us and in society. There are some that we would like in our lives or perhaps feel we should have in our lives. These would not be deemed as our core values.

Do you know what your core values are?

Do the people you coach know what theirs are?

The closer we live our lives in line with our own individual core values, the more positive emotion we feel, such as happiness, fulfilment, satisfaction, calmness. Equally, the further we live our lives from our core values, the more negative emotions we feel, such as sadness, frustration, anger and intense unhappiness.

**Understanding our core values is the first step
to understanding what makes us happy.**

Groups of Values

Values can be classified in many different ways. The way I find most helpful, identifies two main groups of values:

1. **'Outcome Values'** which are those that we are working towards achieving in our lives. These are values such as:

    *   success
    *   happiness
    *   freedom
    *   independence
    *   security
    *   wellbeing
    *   knowledge
    *   peace

2. **'Values for the Journey'** which are the values that are important to the way we live our lives, the guiding principles for our behaviour and decisions.
    These are values such as:

    *   honesty
    *   integrity
    *   loyalty
    *   trust
    *   love
    *   fairness
    *   respect
    *   equality

Our Top 10 core values are likely to include a mixture of both types.

What combination of values do you have?

A similar classification comes from the social psychologist Milton Rokeach[*], who conducted a Values Survey in 1973 and classified values into 'Terminal' and 'Instrumental' values. He described

---

[*] See reference 1

Terminal values as being 'made up of end game values, personal or social, so benefitting you or society'. He described Instrumental values as being those 'that are moral values and competence values, so are modes of behaviour that when violated cause pangs of conscience or feelings of guilt'.

**Live your life with 'Values for the Journey';
let the journey take you on a path to attain your 'Outcome Values'.**

Lindsay West

Levels of Values

Values operate at many different levels, the main ones are:

- Personal values, which are our main focus in this book. These are the values important to an individual and which represent the core of who they are. For any individual these will be made up of a combination of innate values (ones that are natural to us all, like love and security), family values, educational values, cultural values, social values, moral values and possibly religious values.
- Organisational values, which are stated by an organisation as being important to them and which represent what they stand for. In values-driven organisations, these values will be evident in the decisions made by management and in the behaviour and actions of their employees.
- Community or Society values, which are stated as being important to a community or society and by which their members operate.
- National values, which are stated as being important to a nation, as a whole.

At whichever level you focus, the values exist and can be identified. However the question remains as to whether individuals, organisations, communities, societies or indeed nations actually live according to the values they hold.

An ideal world would be one in which everyone understood the values at each level and lived their lives in line with those values, honouring those values with their behaviour, decisions, language and actions.

Do you want to play a part in creating that kind of a world?

By living your values and by coaching one person to understand and live their values you have made a difference. By doing this with many people and in organisations or in the community, just imagine what a difference you could make.

Put values at the heart of society to make the world a better place.

Values and Emotion

Values are not emotions; they are the things that influence emotional responses in us. Whether it be positive emotion when these values are honoured or negative emotion when they are not.

We will feel a positive emotional response when our own thoughts, language and behaviour are aligned to our core values. For example, if we have a core value of kindness, then being kind to someone will make us feel good.

Equally, we will feel a negative emotional response when we dishonour our own values, through how we think, speak or behave. For example, if we have a strong value of honesty, then telling a lie will make us feel bad, regretful or guilty.

The strength of the emotional response depends on:

- the scale of the impact;
- how many values have been impacted;
- the priority of those values to the individual.

The more values affected, the bigger the impact. The higher the priority of the values affected, the stronger the emotion felt by the individual.

Our emotions will also be triggered by the impact something or someone has on our values. If an event or someone's words or actions have a negative impact on one or more of our values, then this will generate a negative emotional response e.g. anger, sadness, disappointment, frustration.

For example, if someone jumps the queue you are in, you might respond in a mildly annoyed way as their actions have dishonoured your value of fairness. However if you witnessed a more serious act of injustice e.g. someone being robbed then this might dishonour several of your values such as fairness, security, respect, trust and so create a much stronger negative emotional response in you, like anger, fear or sadness.

Equally, if an event or someone's words or actions have a positive impact on our values, then a positive emotional response will be felt e.g. happiness, fulfilment. The more values affected and the higher the priority of those values, the bigger the impact and so the bigger the positive emotional response will be.

For example, if you complete a piece of work and get a 'well done' from your boss, it will make you feel good if you have core values of recognition or appreciation. If you complete a project and get an award and a bonus from your company, then your response might be stronger and more emotional as more values are likely to be honoured, if you have core values of recognition, appreciation, respect, achievement, status, for example.

Interestingly, if these values are not important to us, then in that situation the recognition may leave us feeling rather different. We may be left neutral or perhaps even embarrassed if we have a stronger value of humility. Alternatively, the completion of the project may leave us feeling empty or perhaps uncertain, if we have a stronger value of security and don't know what we will be working on next.

By identifying and understanding our values, we can understand where our emotion comes from and this can really help with managing those emotions.

We can draw on the value that has been dishonoured to help us respond in a better way. For example, when we feel bad after telling a lie, due to the impact on our value of honesty, we can then draw on that value of honesty to help us be more truthful in the future. If we didn't realise how important that value was to us, we may not have taken that action and would continue to have felt guilty, without really understanding the impact on ourselves.

Another example might be that if we know the value of wellbeing is really important to us, then we can draw on that value to help us make better decisions about what we eat and about exercising, without the sense of having to do it because others say it's important. When we feel we *ought* to do something, we are much less likely to make it happen and may rebel against those feelings.

Values are important in communication and relationships too. If we understand the values of those around us, this helps us to understand

and manage their emotional responses. We can have much better relationships with people if we understand what is important to them and what makes them tick.

If we honour the values of others with our behaviour and the words we use, then we know it will generate positive emotion and responses from them. Likewise if we dishonour the values of others then we should not be surprised if it causes negative emotion and behavioural responses from them.

We do not have to have the same set of values to be in a good relationship with someone, however it is very helpful if we understand and honour each other's values in the way we speak and behave, even if our values are quite different.

For example, to enhance a personal or a business relationship with someone who has a core value of appreciation, you can honour their value just by showing appreciation for what they do. Of course, it needs to be sincere and earned. The key here is remembering to verbalise it and let them know they are appreciated.

Which of your values generate the most positive emotion in you and which generate the most negative emotion?

Do you know how to use your values to manage your emotion?

In Part 2, techniques are provided in the 'Awareness of Self and Change Needed' section to help the coachee understand the impact of decisions and events on their values, through the emotions they feel. Then in the 'Managing Emotions' section of 'Living a Values-Led Life', there are techniques to use core values to manage emotional responses, in a range of difficult situations.

Understand which core values have received a negative impact, then draw on those same values to manage your emotional response.

Values and Motivation

Motivation is our desire and enthusiasm to do something and so is a key part of being able to achieve what we want in life. Often a lack of motivation is what holds people back from taking action and putting in the effort to attain their goals.

Values act as our motivators and drivers, so understanding our own motivators helps us to tap into them, when we most need that boost. Linking our goals to our values helps motivate us to make them happen. We can draw on our values to help us achieve things and to help us get through challenges and difficult times.

For example, people who run marathons or do extreme challenges, often do so to raise money for charity. Whilst getting fit is a good by-product of all the relentless training required, the value that many marathon runners draw on for motivation is that they are 'making a difference' to the lives of others with the funds they raise.

It is that feeling that gets them up before the sun, or sends them out in the cold and rain and keeps them going when they hit 'the wall'. This value combined with others, such as achievement, generosity, contribution, kindness, compassion and support can make a powerful combination of motivators to help many people to keep going through extreme levels of adversity.

If there is something you have to do that you do not really want to do e.g. sit an exam or take a driving test, then by linking the task to your values, it can significantly help you to be successful.

You might draw on values of freedom or independence to keep you focused on doing well in a driving test, which would mean you could then get a car and be free to go wherever you want, whenever you want.

By keeping these values in mind, you are focused on the outcome and what it gives you which is very motivating and helps to make even the most unpleasant task more manageable.

When does lack of motivation hold you back?

**When you feel held back, draw on your values
to motivate you to take action and move forward.**

Lindsay West

Values and Behaviour

In order to help someone change their behaviour, it is useful to recognise the difference between values and behaviour and separate the two. All too often people see poor behaviour in others and assume they are bad people. This is a big misconception.

I believe all values are positive and so we all have positive values. However, if our behaviour is not aligned to them, we can let ourselves down. We may be making the wrong choices and being led down the wrong path in life, by external influences. The good news is that behaviour can be changed.

Values are the things that are important to us. They define who we are. Whereas our behaviour is just what we say, do and think and this behaviour may or may not be aligned to our values. The perceptions others have of us, however, are more likely to be based on our language and behaviour, as this is what they observe.

Without awareness of our core values, we may allow our behaviour to be directed by things that are seemingly but not truly important to us e.g. wanting designer clothes or to own a sports car. When behaviour is not aligned to values, people may seem to be acting out of character, or being inconsistent or inauthentic which can be uncomfortable for those on the receiving end.

The more awareness we have of our values the more we can ensure that what we say, do and think, is aligned to and honouring those values. Then we will appear consistent and authentic as we are being our true selves.

A specific example of values generating behaviour which I have observed in my coaching practice is that people with a strong value of security, in the financial aspect of their lives, often need to ensure they have a reserve of funds in the bank. This gives them a contingency and protects them from risk of sudden unforeseen expenditure. If they are not able to have this, even a small overdraft can be very distressing and create great fear of spending on anything except necessities. Maintaining this reserve honours their value of security sufficiently for them to operate in a normal way and spend money on what they want.

The opposite example I have observed, is that people with a strong value of abundance are able to take great financial risks to create more opportunity and wealth. Large debts do not concern them as they focus on the potential for growth of their investments or assets.

Some behavioural profiling systems use sets of generic values that match each personality type and so recognise the part values play in influencing behaviour patterns.

If we are aware of our values and live our lives according to them, then our behaviour will match and honour our values and we will feel happy and fulfilled as a result.

However, if we do not understand or are not aware of our values, or are not behaving in alignment with and honouring them, then we are very likely to be feeling unhappy and unfulfilled.

For example, if someone has a strong value of honesty, they might occasionally find themselves in a position where they feel they have to say something that is not true. This will make them very uncomfortable and possibly unhappy if it continues for a period of time, as their behaviour is acting against their core value. By finding a way to be more honest in the situation, it will give them a huge sense of relief, as they will be acting in line with their value once again.

People often ask me if it is possible to change the values of someone else. My response to this is always no and neither should they try, because a person's values are at the heart of who they are. In my view, values are always positive, it is behaviour we need to address. So actually what people want to change is the behaviour of others and this is again why understanding the difference between values and behaviour is so important.

No-one has bad values, just sometimes bad behaviour. So we need to support others in changing their behaviour not their values. Encouraging others to behave in alignment with their values will significantly improve their quality of life.

A good example here is that of a criminal. People may judge them as a bad person or someone with bad values, whereas actually it is the way they behave that is being judged.

A thief may have positive values of independence and freedom or perhaps they want to provide for their families, there is nothing bad in that. However if they choose to steal from others, rather than earning the money themselves, this is the bad behaviour by which they are judged. It's not their values that are bad, just the choices they have made in trying to honour them.

It is likely that their negative behaviour is dishonouring other values they may have, such as honesty, so they will not feel happy as a result of honouring one value only to dishonour another.

Some people may see the value of power as bad. However, my view is that power in itself is not bad, it is a positive value. Without key people having this as a core value, we might never have key world leaders, who thrive in positions of power. It is only when people abuse their power with poor behaviour that there is a problem.

Does your behaviour always honour your values?

How does it feel, when it does not?

To live our lives in line with our core values, we need to be making decisions and choices that honour all these individual values. We need to be behaving in a way that supports our values. We need to be operating in an environment where those around us behave in a way that honours our values too. This ensures that we will feel happier and more fulfilled, as we are being true to ourselves.

Separate your values from your behaviour,
honour your values and change your behaviour.

Values and Beliefs

Understanding the difference between values and beliefs can be crucial in unlocking potential and overcoming the barriers to success. Confusing the two could mean you try to change the wrong one. Having certainty of which to change gives better clarity and focus.

Values are very different from beliefs. Both are often formed in our early years of life, through the influence from family, friends and teachers etc. Our values are positive and core to who we are and do not change much throughout our lives.

Beliefs, however, are convictions or assumptions; things we believe to be true and they can be positive and negative. They can be helpful or limiting and they can be adopted, changed or dropped very easily. There are many coaching and NLP techniques to support people in changing limiting beliefs.

To explain the difference between values and beliefs, a person who has a value of honesty may have a positive belief that supports this value e.g. 'honesty is the best policy' or a negative or limiting belief that does not e.g. 'the truth hurts'.

The positive belief is likely to lead to behaviour of being honest and speaking the truth, which honours the value of honesty. Whereas, the limiting belief which may have been adopted as a result of an unpleasant experience in the past, may lead to behaviour that limits their honesty, perhaps by telling people what they want to hear, rather than the truth, as they feel this is kinder.

This belief does not support the value of honesty and if this behaviour is continued, it may cause a negative emotional response, such as frustration, sadness or unhappiness. So behaviour caused a limiting belief, such as being unable to speak freely for fear of hurting someone, could lead to dishonouring the value.

Another example might be someone with a core value of kindness. A supporting belief might be 'what goes around comes around' i.e. if I am kind to others, they will be kind to me. A limiting belief might be 'you have to be cruel to be kind' which might generate unkind behaviour that does not support the value at all.

In Neuro Linguistic Programming (NLP), values have the same meaning as I have described i.e. why we behave the way we do, what is important to us. However, in NLP it seems that values tend to be grouped together with beliefs and attitudes, in terms of contributing factors to understanding people's patterns of thoughts, feelings and behaviours. NLP practitioners sometimes suggest that values, beliefs and attitudes can and need to be changed to break unhelpful behaviour patterns or mindsets.

My thoughts here are that unhelpful or limiting beliefs and attitudes can and need to be changed to support the desired behavioural adjustment. Values, however, are the fundamentals of life for an individual and so cannot easily be directly changed or enforced in the same way.

I have come across examples of programmes where participants are encouraged to adopt a set of values to become high achievers and thus high earners. Whilst this approach may have some short term benefits in generating certain kinds of behaviours, it is unlikely to be sustainable.

Acting against our core values is not only uncomfortable and inauthentic but likely to be damaging if continued for a period of time, as the growing negative emotion builds into stress.

Do your beliefs support your values?

Beliefs may come and go, but your values are here to stay.

Values and Principles

Values can sometimes be defined as principles. Oxforddictionaries. com definition of values is 'Principles or standards of behaviour; one's judgement of what is important in life'. Therefore, it is useful to have clarity on their differences and similarities.

Principles can be viewed as fundamental truths or a common understanding of how things should be. Values are the principles that are important to us, as individuals, which drive our choices and behaviours and generate our emotions. Not all principles are values and not all values are principles.

We may live our lives according to a set of principles and as long as these are ones we choose because they are the things that are important to us then they are likely to be the same as our values.

The difficulty comes if we try to live our lives according to a set of principles drawn up by someone else. Some of those principles may be more meaningful to us than others, so if we try to live our lives in line with all of them, some conflict may arise if we hold other values at a higher priority.

Religious principles are a good example here. Whatever our religion, there is likely to be a set of guiding principles laid out for us, as a way to live our lives. As a follower of that religion, we agree to adopt those principles and honour them daily. Frustration can set in though, if we try to uphold those guiding principles but constantly fail, as we may hold other values, outside of those prescribed by our religion, that are more important to us personally.

For example, a Christian parent knows that patience is a fundamental principle in Christian teaching and every day they may try hard to show patience with their children.

-   They may allow them to continue speaking, when they need them to listen, dishonouring their own value of fairness.
-   They may allow them to finish what they are doing, even when they need them to hurry up, as they are late for school,

dishonouring their own value of reliability/punctuality to arrive on time.

- They talk patiently to them when their behaviour is bad or they are being rude, dishonouring their own value of respect for one's elders.

Faith, for many, includes putting 'higher' principles above their own values and striving to be better people. Clearly with this comes a high degree of effort and no little amount of frustration with frequent challenge and sometimes failure.

In his book 'The 7 Habits of Highly Effective People', Stephen Covey[*] talked about principles as distinct from values. He saw principles as 'natural laws that are woven into the fabric of every civilised society'. He saw them as deep fundamental truths that have universal application and upon which enduring happiness and success are based. In that way, they are indeed the same as values, Covey saw principles as the 'objective reality' and values as the 'subjective version of reality' emerging from an individual's experience and conditioning.

Here are some examples of how Covey saw principles evolving into individual values:

Examples of Covey's principles:		Evolved into individual values:
fairness		sense of equity and justice
integrity, honesty	⟹	sense of trust
service		sense of contribution
quality		sense of excellence
potential		idea that we can develop
growth		releasing potential

Drawn from text of The 7 Habits of Highly Effective People, by S.R.Covey[**]

In essence this is very similar to my view of a values-led life. Establish what is important to you then live your life according to those values. My understanding and definition of values incorporates Covey's principles, rather than differentiating them from values. Principles are the guiding rules outside of us, which we may adopt as our core

---

[*]   See reference 2

[**]   See reference 2

values, interpret and follow in our lives, if they are congruent with what is important to us.

Using the example of fairness, most people recognise the principle of fairness as something to guide how we behave. Most people try to be fair to others and appreciate others being fair to them. So it works as both a principle and a value. It is our life experience that affects how fundamentally important fairness is to us and how strong our emotional response is when we are treated unfairly or see others being treated unfairly. This then determines whether fairness is a core value for us or of lower priority to other values.

Reflect on which principles form core values for you.

It is better to be one who knows and lives by their core values, than just being a principled person.

Values and Morals

In a similar way to principles, morals and values can be used to mean the same thing, however again it is helpful to have clarity of the differences.

Morals are our understanding of what is right and wrong. Ethics, a more popular term used these days, can be seen as the standards by which behaviours are evaluated in society for their morality or rightness and wrongness.

Morals and ethics tend to be enforced on us by external influences, such as our culture, community or society. They are indications of how we 'should' behave. Whereas, values come from within us and they are at the core of our being.

Honouring our core values makes us feel happy and fulfilled, whereas honouring morals tends to produce a more self-righteous feeling. 'Haven't I been good?' is the response to honouring a moral, rather than, 'I feel great', which would be the response to honouring a core value.

Some values might be described as 'moral values' such as decency, duty, honour, faithfulness, integrity, honesty.

Take, for example, the word 'decency'. Most people would view this as a moral, an expected code of conduct and way of behaving in public. If you see someone behaving indecently, even in a minor way, like dropping litter in the street, it can produce a sense of outrage. Yet, if we are decent people and do what we are told, put our litter in the bin and recycle what we are supposed to, then that moral feeling comes into play. We feel we are doing our bit for society and the world.

Decency would only be a core value for someone who really felt a sense of fulfilment from upholding certain standards of behaviour, perhaps someone working in law enforcement.

However, some people enjoy breaking the rules, being rebellious and deliberately stepping over that line of decent behaviour. Morals are seen by them as what certain institutions, e.g. governments, educational or religious organisations, tell them they should be doing. If they reject those institutions, because of their experiences of them, then they may seek pleasure from breaking those codes of conduct. Their own values of excitement, fun, freedom or challenge would prevail.

Do you have any moral values in your Top 10 core values?

A world with morals is a good place; a world with values is a happy place.

Lindsay West

Organisational Values and Personal Values

When choosing a career, it is essential to understand the fit between an organisation's values and your personal values to ensure that it will provide an environment in which you will thrive and not one in which you will struggle to survive.

Without this understanding, costly mistakes can be made in terms of career decisions. People often change organisations because they are not thriving where they are and because they want to develop themselves and grow and improve their knowledge, skills and experience to achieve success.

Many organisations have at some point defined a set of organisational values. The question is, what have they done with them? Do they sit in posters on walls around the company buildings, never looked at and gathering dust? Has that organisation put in place a plan and taken steps to embed those values into the behaviour, processes and culture of its people? Are values part of the performance management system? Is it a truly values-driven organisation or do the management 'espouse' the values as the way the staff should behave, but do not 'walk the talk' themselves?

For example, a company may have customer satisfaction as one of its organisational values. However, in practice if decisions are always made, and results rewarded, based on profit rather than being customer focused, it is likely that the value is not embedded into the essence of that organisation.

It is helpful to understand an organisation's values before applying to work for them to ensure a good fit with your own personal values. It is also beneficial to spend time with staff to understand how well those values are reflected in their behaviour within the company.

For example, a client came to me wanting a career change. She described her employer to me as a third sector, not-for-profit, organisation which has 'learning and development' as one of its core values and describes itself as a 'learning organisation'. It has an environment where there is great focus on learning and development and lots of opportunities for growth. However, a belief system, within the culture of the company, has developed whereby it is felt that there is 'always more to learn'. This has led to behaviour where no-one can ever be seen or recognised as an expert or be valued for an academic achievement.

She was attracted to work in the organisation because of its core values, which seemed to be a good fit with her own. However once working there the behaviours that have evolved are stifling that learning and dishonouring those values. It is a very frustrating work environment for someone who has values of knowledge, learning, achievement and recognition.

However hard she tries, she will never be good enough to be recognised as an expert or someone who has achieved a certain degree of knowledge in their field, to be respected and looked up to by colleagues. The culture in the organisation simply will not allow it and has come to ridicule any attempts by staff to set themselves up as experts. Needless to say, she has since left the organisation.

Just as it is crucial that individuals keep a constant check on whether their behaviours are in line with and are honouring their own core personal values, so it is with organisations. They must ensure that the developing culture, systems and processes and the behaviours of staff all continue to honour the core values of the organisation, so it remains a values-driven organisation.

When looking at organisational values, you would not expect a company to have exactly the same kind of values as an individual. However, some correlation between the values of a company and its staff is beneficial. For example, some people choose to work for an organisation purely because of the values they uphold e.g. diversity, accessibility, social responsibility.

Organisational values often include words such as innovation, customer service, collaboration, integrity, professionalism and quality.

Someone with core values of creativity and challenge may seek out companies with the value of innovation, so they have the opportunity to work in an environment where they can thrive.

People with strong values of justice, fairness and equality may seek careers in law, law enforcement or perhaps human rights organisations.

Those for whom learning and development are important values may choose a career in education, coaching or mentoring.

The same is true for smaller groups, such as Neighbourhood Watch and local voluntary organisations. These are filled with people who value a sense of community and contribution.

> *What are the Values of your organisation or business*
> *and are they in evidence daily in your interactions with*
> *colleagues and clients?*

Work in or create an organisation whose values align to yours and you will thrive, not just survive.

Values and Identity

Who we are and what our purpose is are fundamental questions that people usually ask themselves at some point in their lives. Our identity is a crucial contributor to our sense of self. Without that clarity, we can suffer from low self-esteem, low confidence and a feeling of insignificance.

Identity is about who we are being, our sense of self and purpose or mission in life. Whereas values are the reason why we feel the way we do. They are what motivates us to behave the way we do, make the decisions and choices we do.

An NLP model called Logical Levels is helpful in making this distinction, originally known as Neurological Levels, it was inspired by Gregory Bateson and developed by Robert Dilts* in 1990.

Logical Levels

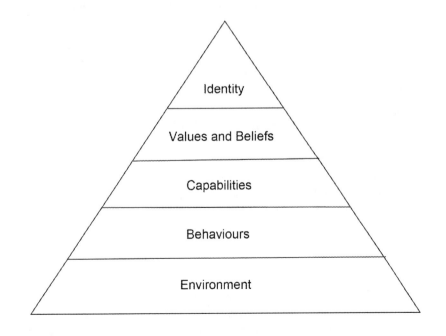

---

*   see reference 3

The Logical Levels framework has five basic levels at which an individual can be 'operating', they are:

- Identity – who someone is being; the sense of self and purpose
- Values and Beliefs – why someone does things; what motivates them
- Capability – how someone does things; the skills and strategies used
- Behaviour – what someone is doing; actions and reactions
- Environment – where and when things are happening; opportunities and constraints

In the framework, values underpin identity, so it is essential that a person's identity is congruent with their values, and vice versa, for them to be effective.

We all have many identities or roles in life e.g. coach, business owner, parent, friend, colleague, customer. Exploring the alignment of identity and values in each role is helpful for raising self-awareness, in particular for understanding why a person feels fulfilled or not.

For example, if a person has a strong value of creativity, but the identity they have or the person they are being doesn't allow for this to be expressed because of the career they've chosen e.g. a banker or an analyst; then they may not feel fulfilled as there is incongruence between their identity and values.

With this awareness, they could focus on enhancing other values that they hold that better support that identity e.g. sense of achievement or security. They could find other identities or roles where their creativity can be expressed, such as through a hobby or in starting their own business.

Alternatively, they could look to change their main identity or role e.g. by changing their job to find one that allows them to express their creativity more freely and thus they will feel more motivated and more fulfilled as a person.

Does your identity align with your core values?

Contemporary examples of the effectiveness of values and identity alignment can be seen in two female celebrities, singer Beyoncé and model Jordan. Interestingly, both have seemingly developed different identities with different sets of values for them to be successful in their different careers.

In TV and Web interviews, Beyoncé talks about her true self as a sensitive, vulnerable and shy person, who developed the separate identity of 'Sasha Fierce' to allow her to perform in her music career. This created identity with its strong sense of sexuality, passion and boldness helps her to perform with the confidence and power she needs to create impact and be successful on stage.

Jordan became successful as a 'Page 3 model'. This identity had a strong sense of sexuality and passion, winning Cover Girl of the Decade (Loaded Award) in 2004. Whereas she launched a later career under her own name Katie Price. She demonstrated values of responsibility, nurturing and contribution as a mother, by sharing her challenges and methods for survival and success, through her web presence and books. She won Celebrity Mum of the Year (Grattan Award) in 2007.

Let your core values define you.

Trust

2. Where do Values come from?

Understanding your personal family history, genetic heritage and your cultural roots provides a significant connection to the past that can enhance people's sense of self and sense of belonging. Without this knowledge, people can feel lost, isolated and disconnected.

It is the same with values. Understanding where your values come from not only enhances your self-awareness but can give a greater sense of connection, significance and belonging. Exploring your values enables you to see which people in your life influenced you to be who you are today.

Two questions I am often asked are: "Where do our values come from?" and "Do they change throughout our lives?" I will address both in this chapter.

Early Years

I believe some values are innate in us, from nature rather than nurture, i.e. from conception, in our genes and part of our personalities, rather than being learned after we have been born.

For example, babies cry when they feel insecure and want attention, so it would seem probable that we are born with basic values of security and love that need to be honoured from the day we are born.

The influences we receive in our early formative years are the source of many of our core values. It is generally accepted that up to about the age of seven, we absorb everything around us and accept much of it as true. We learn values from those around us: our parents, care-givers, close family members and teachers. The values that they instil in us are likely to remain important to us all our lives. Sociologist Morris Massey calls this *The Imprint Period. *

Values adopted in this stage could be ones such as kindness, fun, joy, happiness, friendship, caring, trust, obedience, creativity and adventure.

With which values do you want to inspire others in your life?

Pre-Teens

Between the ages of eight and twelve, we are more aware of the differences between people and we start to copy those around us. These people may be our parents, our teachers, religious or cultural leaders. We try things out to see how they feel, rather than blindly accepting them, as we did in our early years. Massey calls this *The Modelling Period.* *

Values adopted during this stage could be fairness, support, learning, development, recognition, achievement, courage, belonging, loyalty, responsibility, respect, sense of duty and tradition.

At this pre-teen stage, how we experience the values of our care-givers seems to make a big difference in whether we adopt or reject their values. If we have a good experience, then it is likely we will adopt that value ourselves.

For example, a mother of two children wants them both to understand the importance of the value of fairness. She works hard to treat them both fairly and makes a point of being fair at important moments for the children e.g. outings, birthdays and Christmas.

If the children have a good experience of being treated fairly, then it is likely that they will grow up with that value of fairness being important to them in the way they live their lives. They will look to treat others fairly and will expect to be treated fairly by others.

Any instance when they feel unfairly treated will cause a strong negative emotional response in them such as frustration or possibly anger. These responses to unfair situations may continue well into adulthood, if they have adopted fairness as one of their core values.

Religious influences in our childhood can affect our values. Values such as community, charity, generosity, forgiveness and compassion may well be sourced from these environments. These values are unlikely to be lost as we grow into adults, even if practising the religion is less evident in our lives.

If we have a negative experience in relation to someone else's values, then it is much less likely that we will adopt that value ourselves and are much more likely to establish a different core value that we see as more important.

For example, a sense of duty or tradition is important in many cultures. Children may be expected to attend family events, regularly visit or take care of elderly relatives, perhaps even agree to an arranged marriage.

However, if a family insists on their children taking part in events or undertaking actions that they are not comfortable with, this negative experience could lead those children to reject those values of duty and tradition. They may choose to value things they view as the opposite to them, in this case perhaps choice, independence or freedom.

Our educational environment has an impact on our values too. In the UK there is a strong focus on values of learning, development, achievement and recognition, based on results. For example there are SATs from a young age, entrance exams for many secondary schools, Ofsted reports and published exam results. Depending on our experiences in education, these may become important values to us.

Our values are very much influenced by our home, social, religious, cultural and educational experiences, during this period of our lives.

> *Which values became important to you during this period of your life?*

Teens to Twenties

Between the ages of approximately 13 and 21 years, the values of our peers have a major influence on us. As we develop as individuals, we naturally turn to people who seem more like us. Other influences at these ages include the media, society and politics especially those aspects which seem to resonate with the values of our peer groups. Massey calls this *'The Socialization Period'.* [*]

---

[*] See reference 4

Core values adopted during this period could be independence, freedom, choice, acceptance, connection, justice, equality, diversity, honesty, beauty, celebrity and passion.

Examples of media influence:

The media targeting girls in this age group focus on the value of beauty, a natural and wonderful thing. In the past the media have come in for criticism for how they do this and perhaps there is still too much encouragement for vulnerable people to spend money they may not have on products that claim to make them thinner and more beautiful. However, in response to reader pressure there has been a shift in the behaviours of the media from using images of size zero models and airbrushed photos to using more realistic and attainable images of beauty, with more focus on wellbeing and good health.

There are many TV shows that focus on the value of celebrity. Many celebrities use this status as a platform for good in the world, through charity fundraiser events, for example. At the other extreme reality TV shows seem to draw people in, using the potential of attaining celebrity, only to reject them by adopting poor behaviour such as judgement, ridicule and humiliation.

Our values may be influenced through other media too, e.g. books and films. There is an endless supply of 'get rich quick' books, using values of freedom and wealth to market them. Also the genre of 'chick flick' movies and 'chick lit' books, play with values of love, friendship and happiness.

Examples of social influence:

Our values may be influenced by the friends and partners we choose. In relationships with a wider variety of people we may experience different values to those of our closer family and community.

We may indeed choose friends and partners with values we are attracted to that we either share or that we have not experienced before or that perhaps are important to us but have not been honoured by those closer to us in the past.

Friendships tend to deepen during this period of our lives and so become more meaningful as we start to feel our values being truly honoured by those around us. The converse will be true when friendships end.

The 'teenage angst' kicks in here when teenagers feel their newly established core values get 'stomped all over' by people in their lives. For example a fifteen year old who is starting to really value independence, choice and freedom is very likely to express strong negative emotion if their parents are still focused on instilling the values of obedience and trust from their early years!

Examples of political influence:

The UK political arena uses values to attract people to support particular parties. Here are some of the values quoted on the various Party websites. The values of David Cameron's Conservative Party include fairness, trust, shared responsibility and stability. The Labour Party values are stated as social justice, rights and community. The Liberal Democrats' constitution aims for a 'fair, free and open society', balancing the 'values of liberty, equality and community'. UKIP are promoting an independent, free and fair Britain. The Green Party promotes social and environmental justice.[*]

Those in this age group may be influenced by the political views of their peers for example at University campuses, Sixth Form Colleges and some schools where political debating, lobbying or rallying takes place.

As economic, social and political change happens, so does their influence on our individual values. How we experience these changes depends upon their impact on our lives and the significance to us and those around us.

Reflect on your teenage years and the influences on your values.

Adulthood

Our core values are formed throughout our early years, childhood and adolescence; those core values stay with us throughout our lives. There may be some values that we hold but only truly appreciate with

---

[*] See reference 5

maturity as adults. These might be values such as integrity, making a difference, honour, humility, inner peace, authenticity, wellbeing and compassion.

So the question remains as to whether our values change throughout our lives. My view here is that our core values remain important to us all through our lives. What may change in adulthood is the *level* of importance we attach to each value and, as such, the prioritisation we give them.

There are three main factors to consider here:

1. **major life experiences** such as marriage, the birth of a child, redundancy, bereavement, illness or divorce often change our perspective on life and can cause a shift in the level of importance we attach to certain core values.

2. **external influences** may bring certain values into consciousness and so likewise can cause a shift in the level of importance a value has to us individually. Those influences could be things such as wars, natural disasters, economic recession, government policy, societal and cultural shifts, global events, industrial developments e.g. technology.

3. **conscious influencing** which is when we choose to prioritise a particular value that is important to us individually.

1. Major life experiences

As we mature, we develop close friendships and once we start having close relationships, we come to understand better values such as love, friendship, loyalty, trust, support and honesty.

We know when we feel these things in a relationship and we start to learn how important they are to us. Major life events such as marriage or the birth of a child may strengthen these values and so they may increase in priority for us.

Sadly, sometimes we may not realise the full importance of these values to us until something happens that has a major negative impact on them.

The prioritisation we hold for certain values can change substantially on the loss of a partner, whether through bereavement, illness or divorce. For example, if the cause of a break-down in a relationship is a breach of trust, then the importance of this value to the betrayed party is likely to be significantly increased when seeking a new partner.

A person with core values of security and development may feel development is a higher priority to them whilst in a stable job. However, if they were to be made redundant, security is likely to become of extreme importance to them and development perhaps less so, until a new job is found.

2. External Influences

Global and National:

World events that take place and the national culture and societal values that are operating during our lives can all have an impact on the prioritisation we give certain values. Looking back there are some eras that stand out in terms of prevalent national values in the UK:

For example, Victorian society is said to have valued decency, respect, status, wealth, duty and tradition, as a class system prevailed.

In wartime and recession, we see values of security, community and camaraderie prioritised as people pull together to get by and survive difficult times.

The 60s saw a focus on world peace, love and freedom. The 70s focus was less global and more individualistic and focused on choice and equality. The 80s became an era of personal development, achievement, independence, status and success. With technology developments in the 90s and 2000s, innovation, adaptability, knowledge and social connection became more important. Perhaps, with the year on year increases in charitable fundraising, the 2010s will be defined by values of humanity, contribution and responsibility.

Workplace:

As adults, the values of our peers and colleagues in the workplace are a key influence in our lives. Those with whom we spend time may lead our thinking in particular directions and raise our consciousness of particular values.

For example, if we work in the private sector and the people around us value status, power and success, then we may start to find these things more important too. If however we work in the public sector, values of equality, diversity and security may be more prevalent. In the charity and not-for-profit sectors, a focus on values of making a difference, compassion and justice may lead us to re-evaluate what matters most to us.

If we know which values are important to us then they are likely to influence our career sector choices to work with people with similar values. We are likely to be happier in that environment where our values are honoured by the words and behaviours of our colleagues.

Society and Culture:

What is happening in our society and culture has an influence on our values too. The combination of core values we hold may lead to differences in our behavioural responses to these societal and cultural changes.

For example, the value of sense of belonging is important to most of us, whether consciously or unconsciously. Changes in the levels of diversity within the population in areas of the UK have affected people in different ways. For those who also value variety and equality, being part of a more diverse community is comfortable.

However, for those who also value stability, it can be more challenging as they need to have their own community around them to feel a sense of belonging. If too much change is going on around them, they may feel that they do not fit in and this can lead to erosion of their sense of identity and a feeling of loneliness or resentment.

Equally, they may look to their families to supply the kind of stability of identity that the nation, local community, culture or religion perhaps no longer provides for them.

These days, people may have lived in many different countries, may work in companies that operate globally, may have family origins in another continent. The further we migrate from our family home, the greater our need can be to define our roots.

Interestingly, there has been a huge growth in the numbers of people researching their family trees and family history. Much investment has been made to put historic records onto databases so they can be more accessible via the internet. Thousands of people seeking their connection to the past can now create a coherent story of their origins and establish family foundations.

Industrial Developments: Technology

Technological developments in mobile communications, portable devices and social media have made it easier than ever to get in touch with and stay in touch with a very wide network of friends, family and colleagues.

For example, this has had an interesting impact on our value of connection. The constant need to be connected and have people connecting with us seems to have become a high priority for many, particularly younger adults. Individual connections have become high in quantity but perhaps the depth has been lost, as conversations happening by text, email, Twitter and Facebook are so much shorter.

Is the real feeling of connection being lost as we spend less and less time actually in the presence of friends, family and colleagues? Or can we view social media as a convenient way to organise face to face get-togethers and meetings enabling that sense of connection to be deepened?

The Environment

Governments and the media have raised the Nation's consciousness of environmental values over many years. They have encouraged us to prioritise these values and have championed attitudes and behaviours such as 'going green', 'saving our planet' and recycling our daily waste.

For example, the growth in the organic food market was a testimony to these changed behaviours in the 2000s. However once the recession hit, people started to worry about their jobs and about money. The instinctive value of security was naturally re-prioritised once again and behaviour reverted back to buying cheaper food options. The growth of low-cost focused supermarkets such as Lidl and Aldi and the number of charity and 99p shops on our high streets are evidence of this shift in buying behaviour. The demand for low cost products continues to increase and become more accepted in society.

As the economy improves, it remains to be seen whether these 'greener' values will be prioritised once again and behaviour patterns shifted once more.

In the 1960s, Social Psychologist Milton Rokeach conducted research trials to see if it was possible to change people's values. What was indicated from the research he undertook, was that the level of importance a person places on a specific value could be influenced. He did this by showing individuals a set of values common to people who they aspire to be like, thus encouraging them to prioritise those values.

Much marketing and media uses this principle. However, I do believe that for this influence to be sustainable, those values have to have a strong level of importance to the person in the first place.

3. Conscious Influencing

The third factor to consider is that it is possible for people to consciously prioritise their core values. If a person felt that they wanted to enhance a particular core value in their lives they could prioritise it and focus their thoughts, behaviour and language towards honouring that value over others, for a period of time.

I have found through coaching that people can choose to change the importance they place on particular values to have a direct effect on how they want their lives to be. The caveat here is that the value does have to be important to them in the first place, otherwise the influence is not sustainable.

For example, if a person feels they are overweight or out of shape, then provided wellbeing is an important value to them, they could prioritise it by making choices that enhance that value over others. So they might go to the gym rather than watching TV on three nights a week. In this way they would be prioritising the value of wellbeing over perhaps relaxation. As their wellbeing improves, they might then look at ways to relax doing something active, so they can enhance both values.

Another example could be someone who has been through a relationship break-up when their value of trust has been dishonoured by their partner. That value of trust will have high importance to them in a new relationship. However, through fear of being hurt again their behaviours may be leading them to avoid getting involved with someone. In time, they may find that they want to make a change if they really want a new partner. The value of love may be low in their Top 10, perhaps because they do not feel lovable after what has happened.

To change this situation, they could focus on prioritising the value of love and think about ways to bring love into their lives again. This may mean reducing the level of priority placed on the value of trust, as they will need to take a leap of faith to love someone when they have no way of knowing whether they can trust them 100%.

What can then happen is that once they are able to love again, the trust in that new partner happens naturally and so things equalise. Once the feeling of being loved and loving another is restored and indeed being able to love oneself once more, then it is likely that the value of love will stay at a high priority level as it remains important.

In summary, our core values are formed throughout our early years and childhood through into our early twenties. Those values stay with us throughout our lives. What may change in adulthood is the level of importance we attach to each value and this may be influenced by life experiences, external factors or indeed our own conscious decision.

Reflect on changes to the prioritisation of your values during adulthood?

**Understanding our values helps us to affirm ourselves
in both the present and the past.**

Respect

3. Why are Values Important in Life and Coaching?

Most of us want to be happier even if we are happy already. Happiness is such an individual feeling. What makes one person happy may not make another person happy but we each know when we feel it and when we do not. Once found we want more of it in our lives.

Often people feel unhappy without really knowing why. Sometimes we think we know and make a change and don't feel any different, because we haven't found the root cause of the unhappiness.

Understanding our individual core values gives us a blueprint, a framework, a foundation for happiness. Our core values are the things that need to be present in our lives for us to feel happiness. We each have a unique combination of prioritised values and they are the key to our individual happiness. Honouring these values in the way we think, speak and act in our daily lives substantially increases our levels of happiness.

Doing fewer things that conflict with our core values can reduce our stress levels and benefit our overall health. When we are happy and working in an environment that is good for us, we are more productive and have greater potential to thrive and be more successful.

It is important for us, as coaches, to understand our own values and live those values in our daily lives, so we are being authentic and true to ourselves. When we are coaching, we can behave in alignment with our values, however we must ensure that we do not influence those we coach inappropriately. When exploring values, it is crucial that the coachee finds exactly the right word that resonates for them.

As coaches, the key challenge for us is to help those we coach to understand and live by their core values in order to achieve the happiness and success that is right for them.

In using the values of the coachee to help them set goals, make better decisions, manage their emotions and solve problems, we are passing on techniques which will impact the coachee long after our sessions have finished.

The effects of living a values-led life can be immediate, the changes are sustainable and the positive difference can be life-long.

How does living life in line with our values make a difference?

Clarity and Self-Awareness

Understanding our own core values gives us a sense of who we really are. It helps us to understand our lives, why we made the decisions we did and why we feel the way we do. This self-awareness helps us to feel more secure and grounded.

"It's not hard to make decisions when you know what your values are."
Roy Disney

Values help us to be authentic. They guide us in behaving and communicating in ways that align with what is important to us. That authenticity makes us more attractive and easier to be around. We are more consistent and more 'real' in our interactions with others.

Goal-Setting

Setting a goal without knowing whether achieving it will make us happy means that we could waste a lot of time and energy. Our uncertainty may hold us back from taking action to achieve the goal.

Using our core values to set our goals gives us the certainty that the change will be good for us and that achieving the goals will give us happiness and fulfilment.

Imagine climbing a ladder to get to the top of a tall building and after all the effort and time it has taken, you get to the top only to find that your ladder is up against the wrong building. Understanding and using your core values in setting your goals makes sure that your ladder is up against the right building in the first place and that achieving your goal has the potential to make you happy.

Understanding and Managing Emotions

Using our core values, we can understand and manage our emotions more effectively and respond appropriately in challenging situations.

We feel good, positive emotion e.g. joy, peace, contentment when our values are honoured. The more values that receive a positive impact, the happier and more fulfilled we feel.

We feel strong negative emotion e.g. anger, sadness, frustration, when our values are being 'stomped all over'. The more our values receive a negative impact, the more unhappy we feel.

If we are acting in conflict with our values we feel stressed. The more values affected, the more stressed we feel. To reduce this stress, we need to start honouring our values again.

Understanding which values are receiving impact helps us to understand what is driving our emotions. Drawing on those same values helps us to respond in a measured and appropriate way.

Honouring our values in the way we behave to ourselves and others ensures we keep control of our emotions and break unhelpful reactive behaviour patterns that cause us to make situations worse.

Values are our motivators to make the changes needed in our lives and achieve our goals. By honouring our core values in the way we communicate and behave, our personal confidence and self-esteem increases as we start to trust our ability to respond well and act in a way that is true to who we are.

Decision-Making, Problem-Solving and Taking Action

Values support decision-making. Using our core values with every choice we make and with every action we take, ensures we are making the right choices. We become more effective as we waste less time doing the wrong things.

"The more choices you have, the more your values matter."
Michael Schrage

By exploring problems and understanding the impact they have on our core values, we can quickly find solutions that will help us to feel better about the situation. Taking action is easier when we know it will enhance our values.

Communication and Relationships

We can share what is important to us by making others aware of our core values. By taking the time to understand *their* values, we can understand what is important to them. In so doing, we can significantly improve our relationships by communicating at a deeper level and honouring each other's values.

This is useful for improving both our personal and our business relationships. We become more attractive to others if we are consistent in our communication and we can connect more deeply using values-based language.

In summary, values provide a foundation from which we can transform our lives and a sustainable approach to enable long-lasting happiness, success and personal fulfilment.

Coaching with Values

I have been integrating values into my coaching practice for many years and have been genuinely astounded at the difference it makes to clients, both in terms of speed of change and positive, lasting impact.

Some coach training companies teach coaches how to help coachees to identify their values. However the extent to which coaches then use those values varies widely.

Whilst some coaches may never have been trained to consider values, others do establish a coachee's core values, either in a specific session or whenever they happen to be mentioned. They may refer back to those core values when setting goals and planning action. Many, however, may not feel confident using values as an integral part of their coaching as they lack a clear process for doing so.

It is my experience that putting values at the centre of coaching techniques is the most effective and efficient way to achieve results. I believe values are underutilised in coaching practice and that rather than using values as a check to keep coachees on track, we need a process that starts with values and puts values at the heart of our coaching.

In Part 2, I have detailed a full coaching programme, with processes and values-based techniques which you can use with the people you coach. You can follow the full end-to-end programme or dip in and use specific techniques for particular situations. I would recommend that the 'Values Exploration' step is completed before using the techniques in the later steps of the framework.

More information on workshops and training courses to learn and practise these techniques, can be found on my website: www.valuescoach.co.uk

How could you use values to enhance the benefits for those you coach?

Understanding and living our values benefits our emotional, mental, physical and spiritual wellbeing.

Challenge

Summary of Part 1

Understanding our core values is the first step
to understanding what makes us happy.

Live your life with 'Values for the Journey';
let the journey take you on a path to attain your 'Outcome Values'.

Put values at the heart of society to make the world a better place.

Understand which core values have received a negative impact,
then draw on those same values to manage your emotional response.

When you feel held back, draw on your values
to motivate you to take action and move forward.

Separate your values from your behaviour,
honour your values and change your behaviour.

Beliefs may come and go, but your values are here to stay.

It is better to be one who knows and lives by their core values,
than just being a principled person.

A world with morals is a good place; a world with values is a happy place.

Work in or create an organisation whose values align to yours and
you will thrive, not just survive.

Let your core values define you.

Understanding our values helps us to affirm ourselves
in both the present and in the past.

Understanding and living our values benefits our
emotional, mental, physical and spiritual wellbeing.

Part 2:

The I-VALUE Coaching Framework

Part 2

The I-VALUE Coaching Framework

Some coaches use a framework for their coaching practice, others prefer to be led by their coachees. Some people like structure and process, others prefer a more natural flow. Many coaches draw from a wide range of techniques, others have less experience.

Part 2 of this book details the I-VALUE Coaching methodology, providing a comprehensive framework and set of techniques to enable any coach, or person using coaching, to work with a coachee, using a values-based approach.

It provides a complete end-to-end coaching framework for those who want it. Alternatively those who prefer less structure can dip in and out, choosing particular techniques to suit their needs. There is a wealth of information, tips, case studies and examples to support both approaches.

I   Issue Identification

The framework starts with the coach exploring the issues, needs or problems presented by the coachee. The coachee is the person being coached whether it is a client, colleague or a member of staff.

V   Values Exploration

The next step is when the coach explores values with the coachee, helping them to identify their Top 10 individual core values, which are then prioritised and scored.

A   Awareness of Self and Change Needed

At this point, a time of reflection is needed to help the coachee use the new knowledge of their values to raise their self-awareness and identify the changes they want to make in their lives.

L   Living a Values-Led Life

A range of techniques are provided in this step, for the coach to use, to support the coachee in living a values-led life. These include learning to use values for goal-setting, managing emotions and making change.

Many aspects that people find challenging are covered, including enhancing motivation, increasing confidence and self-esteem, reducing stress, decision-making, prioritising, problem-solving and action planning.

This step may require several sessions, depending on the number of aspects of their lives there are, in which the coachee wants to make change.

U   Understanding the Values of Others

Understanding the values of others, and the importance of this in communication and relationships, is addressed in this step of the framework. Again, this may take several sessions depending on the number of different relationships on which the coachee wants to focus.

E   Evaluating Progress

The framework ends with reflection and evaluation of the progress made.

It is based on a six session coaching programme, however as mentioned above at least two of the steps may well require further focus in additional sessions, depending on the needs of the coachee.

The I-VALUE Coaching Framework

A values-based approach to coaching.

I   Issue Identification

V   Values Exploration

A   Awareness of Self and Change Needed

L   Living a Values-Led Life

U   Understanding the Values of Others

E   Evaluating Progress

I   Issue Identification

The first step of the I-VALUE Coaching Framework is when the coach develops their relationship with their coachee, by building rapport, hearing their story and showing they understand their challenges. At this point trust is deepening between coach and coachee.

Without this step, it may be hard for the coachee to feel they can be open and honest about their situation. Also, if the coachee is unable to 'tell their story' upfront, they may feel the need to keep mentioning their past in later sessions, when their focus really needs to be on moving forwards.

The 'I' step: Issue Identification is therefore a crucial first step in the Framework, as the coach begins by identifying the issues, needs or problems that the coachee brings for coaching.

As coaches, we take those we coach from where they are now to where they want to be, so gaining that initial understanding of where they are now is essential. By careful questioning, attentive and active listening and by showing understanding, a good rapport can be established quickly, building the trust in the relationship.

For coaches, it is important to limit the time that coachees talk about their past in coaching sessions, to avoid crossing the line into counselling. The questions asked at this stage need to bring clarity on the issue, identifying relevant factors, beliefs, behaviour patterns etc. so the coach then knows how best to support the coachee.

The two techniques in this first step of the Framework are both used in the first session of the coaching programme with the coachee, to get a good understanding of their situation. They will give a broad picture of how things are and help to identify specific areas for change.

They can be used with any individual requesting coaching, whether they want to improve upon an aspect of their lives or whether they are presenting an issue, at home or work, with which they are unhappy. They can be used with a member of staff wanting self development or raising a problem they have in the workplace either with their role or in their interaction with other people.

Lindsay West

Examples of issues that may be raised are:

Home:

- need to improve work/life balance;
- need for purpose or direction in life;
- behaviour pattern that needs to change;
- barriers or beliefs holding them back;
- low self-esteem or confidence;
- loss of identity (e.g. in dedicating life to raising children or homemaking);
- relationship issues;
- managing emotions;
- unhappy with life;
- no boundaries and can't say 'no' to people who take advantage.

Work:

- high stress levels, too much pressure, conflict of priorities, compromise of values;
- improve work relationships;
- improve in aspects of work;
- unfair treatment;
- 'stuck in a rut';
- wants promotion/career change;
- loss of self-confidence;
- being bullied;
- time management.

The first technique involves reviewing all relevant aspects of the person's life, to establish all the areas with which they are unhappy and where they want to make some change.

The second technique provides a series of questions. The main purpose is to develop the coach's understanding of the coachee, their preferences, behaviour patterns, level of self-esteem, limiting beliefs and current circumstances.

From this information the coach will then determine how they can best support their coachee, i.e. what approach to use with them and which techniques would suit them best.

At the end of this step in the process, the coach will have a better understanding of their coachee's situation and will have clearly identified the issues faced by the coachee that they have decided to focus on and the changes needed.

This first coaching session will usually last 60 minutes.

How long do your coachees spend talking about their past in coaching sessions?

How do you know when you've engaged rapport and gained the trust of your coachee?

Seek first to understand, then you will be understood.

Issue Identification Technique 1: The Wheel of Life

Overview:

This is a technique widely used by coaches for exploring different aspects of a coachee's life and to identify areas which are out of balance. It develops a focus on the issues arising that they would like to address through coaching.

The Wheel of Life represents the level of satisfaction an individual has with each area of their life, in a wheel format. In a perfect world, balance and satisfaction would give 10's all around the wheel and thus the individual would be fully satisfied in all aspects of their life and be 'having a smooth ride'. The reality is rather different for most people.

This exercise helps to focus on the areas that are out of balance and the areas with lower levels of satisfaction than would be preferred. This can then be used as a basis for change to take into the next step of the process.

Inputs:

- Coach provides Wheel of Life template

- Coachee brings the current view of their life and any issues they identify.

Outcomes:

- Improved understanding of the situation

- Better clarity of the aspects of their life that are out of balance and the specific issues to focus on in future coaching sessions.

Timing:

This exercise is usually completed in the first coaching session and takes between 5-10 minutes. It may take longer if the coachee uses the opportunity to explain the reasons for their scores and shares his/her life story.

Tone:

Coach uses an enquiring and curious tone and remains non-judgemental by accepting the scores given and not passing comment on them or on the shape of the coachee's Wheel. No comparison should be made to other coachee's Wheels.

Note:

When choosing the first aspect of life to score, avoid one that may be a difficult area for the coachee e.g. if you know they are having relationship issues, avoid that aspect first and start with something neutral, like health and fitness.

People do not always know what 'Physical Environment' means; explain this as 'the environment you live/work in'.

Sometimes, people want to give different scores for family and friends, so you can split these out and add another line on the wheel. Also you can add lines for other aspects of their life, not covered, e.g. spirituality.

Technique Process:

Ask the coachee to mark each category on a scale of 0-10, to reflect their level of satisfaction with each area of their life right now. The centre of the wheel is 0 (low satisfaction with that aspect) and the outer edge is 10 (high satisfaction).

Then join each mark with a line to the mark for the next category, to form the individual wheel of their life.

Ask them to reflect on the scores given and identify the areas they are happy with and the aspects they are not happy with i.e. those for which they would like to increase their satisfaction levels.

This technique will identify the aspects of a person's life in which they want to make changes and will give some indication of the issues arising.

Coach: *'This is the Wheel of Life technique, which helps us to see areas of imbalance in your life that you would like to address in our sessions. Give me a number, on the scale of 0-10 for how satisfied you are with each aspect of your life. 0 being 'not at all' and 10 being 'completely satisfied'. Let's start with Health & Fitness.'*

The coachee might say: *'That's about a 5. I want to lose a few pounds and I need to deal with a health issue.'*

Action for the coach: Put a large dot halfway down the line titled Health & Fitness and write a 5 next to it. Then note down 'lose a few pounds and health issue', in the space outside their Wheel by that aspect.

Action for the coach: Then repeat the process for each aspect around their Wheel. Then join each dot to the next to form a shape within their Wheel.

Coach: *'I will leave you to draw your own conclusions from the size and shape of your wheel and how comfortable a ride through life you are having at the moment'*. Allow a moment for reflection, then ask: *'Now could you tell me, which of these scores you would like to increase and what to?'*

The coachee might say: *'I would like to increase Health & Fitness from a 5 to an 8'*

Action for the coach: Capture the chosen aspects, current and target scores on the lines below their Wheel in the template. Use these aspects for the focus of future coaching sessions.

A blank template and an example completed template are shown.

Wheel of Life Template

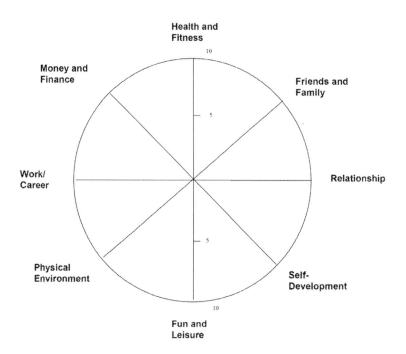

Health and
Fitness

Money and
Finance

Friends and
Family

Work/
Career

Relationship

Physical
Environment

Self-
Development

Fun and
Leisure

Mark each line on the scale of 1-10, in terms of your satisfaction with that area of your life (1 is low, 10 is high), then join each mark to the next to show the wheel of your life. Then reflect on how smooth a ride you are having right now and in which areas of your life you would like to make changes to increase your satisfaction levels.

Area for Change: Current Score: Target Score:

                      Date: Date:

Wheel of Life Example

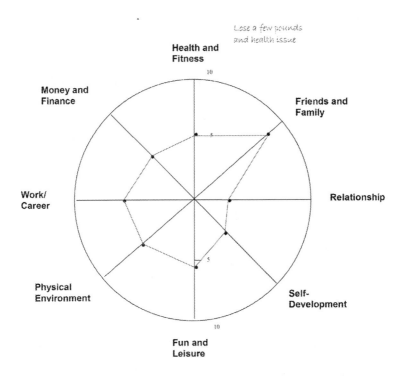

Mark each line on the scale of 1-10, in terms of your satisfaction with that area of your life (1 is low, 10 is high), then join each mark to the next to show the wheel of your life. Then reflect on how smooth a ride you are having right now and in which areas of your life you would like to make changes to increase your satisfaction levels.

Area for Change:	Current Score: Date: xx/xx/xx	Target Score: Date:
Health and Fitness	5	8
Relationship	3	8
Self Development	4	8

Issue Identification Technique 2: Exploration Questions

Overview:

Some coaches use a standard set of questions to explore what is going on with a coachee, at the first session. These are the questions I recommend to give a good understanding of the coachee's situation, state of mind, level of self-esteem, behaviour patterns, beliefs, barriers and specific issues that they want to work on and make progress with. It is important to listen attentively and show your understanding of what is being said.

Inputs:

- The coach asks the questions below, in the session

- The coachee brings their perception of their life, their 'story', their preferences, behaviour patterns, beliefs, expectations and issues or aspects to change.

Outcomes:

- Clear identification of the problems or issues held by the coachee

- Improved understanding of the situation

- Clarification of the most useful coaching style for the coach to use

- Identification of unhelpful behaviour patterns, limiting beliefs, negative mindsets and level of self-esteem of the coachee.

Timing:

This exploration can take between 30-60 minutes depending on how forthcoming or concise the coachee is in their answers. The first eight questions are the essential ones to complete; the others are helpful to give a fuller picture, if there is time. Allow the coachee time to think before answering each question.

Tone:

The coaches tone is enquiring, curious and interested, it is important to remain non-judgemental.

Note:

Watch the coachee's body language, 'mirror' to create rapport, notice any confusion at a particular question and reflect that back to the coachee and perhaps ask the question in a different way. Note down what you hear in respect of beliefs or behaviours etc. to work on e.g.

'No matter how hard I try I will never be successful' indicates a limiting belief and low self-esteem.

'Every man I pick lies to me' indicates a negative mindset, unhelpful behaviour patterns and a limiting belief. Words used like *'always, never, should, ought, try'* can be signs of low self-esteem.

A coachee may also feel they want to give a little more detail of their past if it is relevant to the issue that they want to change. Allow them to tell their 'story' at this point, as it helps to know this background information when doing the next stage of values identification. Listen and show understanding at all times.

Technique Process:

The coach asks:

What are you expecting from the coaching relationship?

How would you like to be coached?

Note: People can find this question hard to answer, it may help to say: *'on a spectrum, where one end is challenging and the other is supportive, where would be the style that would most suit you?'*

How committed are you to change?

How are you about doing what you say you'll do?

What do you want to accomplish through coaching?

What are your ambitions/dreams in life?

How do you limit yourself in life? Where do you get stuck?

How do you deal with:

- *success?*
- *disappointments?*
- *failure?*

In the last 12 months, what have been your biggest:

- *accomplishments?*
- *disappointments?*
- *lessons?*

What are your natural gifts and abilities?

What activities do you enjoy the most?

What aspect(s) do you enjoy least/most about your work? (If appropriate)

Note: The coach can ask: *'What else?'* after any answer, if they believe there is more to hear.

Wellbeing

V   Values Exploration

Once the issues for coaching have been identified, the next step in the Framework is the key to the whole coaching programme.

You will help the coachee to understand what is truly important to them, which will give them a foundation for happiness and success for the rest of their lives.

Without this step, the coachee will have less certainty of whether they are making the right choices, on both major and minor issues. They may continue to procrastinate or make the wrong decisions for them, thus wasting time and energy and causing unnecessary stress in their lives. They may stay unhappier for longer.

The 'V' step in the I-VALUE Coaching Framework is for Values Exploration.

This step is a continuation of the exploration process to understand more about the coachee and for them to understand more about themselves, by identifying their core values.

Most people have some understanding of what values are, however very few people know which values are the most important ones to them.

So this step dedicates a full coaching session to explaining what values are to the coachee and exploring what is important to them across all aspects of their lives. They then refine the list and define their individual prioritised Top 10 core values.

I believe that by helping people gain this amount of clarity, we can make a huge difference to their lives.

Two techniques for helping the coachee to explore and identify their individual core values are included in this section. The choice of technique depends on how much time is available and whether the physical environment is appropriate should the coachee become emotional during the process e.g. in the workplace.

Both techniques may be used if the coachee is finding it hard to think of values that are important to them.

A further two techniques are described to prioritise the values in order of importance to them, at this point in time, in their lives. A visualisation exercise or a simple sorting exercise can be used, again depending on time available and the coachee's preferences.

Finally, a measurement technique is outlined that enables the coachee to score, out of ten, how closely they are living their life in line with each value.

They then review those scores and note a target score for each value that they would like to enhance in their lives. These target scores will be used later in the coaching process when setting goals.

At the end of this step in the process, the coachee will have clearly identified their core set of values, prioritised them and scored them in terms of how closely they are living their life in alignment with those values.

They will also have identified areas with issues arising, where change or improvement is needed.

A full values exploration, prioritisation and measurement session usually takes between 60-90 minutes. Timing will vary depending on which combination of techniques are used and the coachee's understanding of values.

The techniques are described here, if you would welcome some practise in using the techniques in a safe and supported environment, before using them in your own work, then please contact me through www.valuescoach.co.uk to book your place on a Values Coach Training Programme.

Could you make a bigger difference, if you helped every person you coach to understand their core values?

**'Values are like fingerprints, nobody's are the same
but you leave 'em all over everything you do.' Elvis Presley**

Values Exploration Technique 1: Questioning

Overview:

This technique explores a person's values using a questioning process. It will establish the Top 10 core values, most important to an individual. These will be the things that will bring them happiness and fulfilment when honoured, and sadness, frustration and anger when missing or dishonoured in their lives. As they identify each value, you may see the coachee experiencing related emotions in the session.

Inputs:

- The coach brings a knowledge of values and the set of questions to the session

- The coachee knows what is important to them, but is likely to have little understanding of their core values.

Outcomes:

- The coach works with the coachee to produce a set of 10 values that are core to what is important to the coachee

- This list of 10 values should give the coachee a feeling of 'me on a page' in that it will summarise the core of who they are and what is important to them

- The values from this technique will then be used in the prioritisation technique, to establish the order of their importance.

Timing:

The questioning part of the Values Exploration process takes around 40 minutes and would be completed in the second coaching session.

Allow the coachee time for reflection at the end to ensure they have chosen exactly the right words to reflect what is important to them.

Tone:

The coach's tone is enquiring, encouraging and authoritative. The coachee will expect the coach to be knowledgeable on whether a word is a value or not. They may also look to the coach to help them find the right word, so offering some encouraging input and options may be helpful.

Note:

The exploration and elicitation of a person's values can take them to deep levels of emotion. It is therefore quite usual for the coachee to show some expression of emotion during this technique e.g. crying, anger and frustration when they recall specific events that affected their values. Strong emotional responses are a good indicator that they have identified a core value and so are welcomed; ensure the coachee feels supported if this happens.

Technique Process:

The coach uses questions to help the coachee to think about what is important to them and come up with all their core values. From these the Top 10 are then selected.

To ensure every aspect of the coachee's life is explored, the coach can work around each heading from the Wheel of Life technique in the Issue Identification step of the I-VALUE Coaching Framework. The relationships, work and fun and leisure aspects are particularly good for finding values.

Ask the coachee to think about each aspect of their life and ask them the following questions over and over to go deeper and deeper to find the core value. Ask them to choose the word that resonates most with them and is most meaningful.

The coach notes down every value mentioned in the session.

Questions to ask to explore and elicit important values:

Coach:

Relationships

'What do you value in relationships with other people? Think of specific individuals and what you value about them?' Note: this is usually an easy question to get started.

'What is important in this aspect of your life? Note: Refer to each aspect from their Wheel of Life.

Work

'What do you value in your work? What does it give you? What do you get out of it?' Note: This is particularly relevant if the coachee is focusing on a work-related situation or issue.

Fun and Leisure

'What does doing this hobby/activity give you? What is important about it to you?' Note: This question can produce more unusual values and is worth exploring.

Health

'What does good health give you?' Note: Health in itself is not a value, this question takes the coachee to a level deeper, see below for examples.

Money

'What does having more money give you?' Note: Money in itself is not a value, explore what money gives them.

Environment

'What is important about your environment to you?' Note: People's environment does have an effect on them, so this question may produce some interesting values.

What else?

Keep asking, *'What else?'* after each question above, until you are sure you have reached the base value and they are unable to come up with any more.

Other aspects

If you are aware of any other aspects of the coachee's life that has not been covered e.g. spirituality or a particular interest or sport they follow, then ask:

'Are there any other aspects of your life that you would like to focus on that may give us some other values?'

Children

If the coachee has children, you might ask:

'What values do you feel are important to nurture in your children?'

Negative emotion

Another useful approach to take is for the coach to explore the causes of negative emotion by asking:

'What makes you angry/sad/frustrated?', then ask,

'What is the positive opposite value that is missing in that situation?'

(See more examples of questions to elicit positive values from negative emotion after this technique. These are particularly useful when working with a coachee with low self-esteem.)

Always allow the coachee to choose the positive opposite value. Bear in mind that they might not choose the word you would expect. E.g. the opposite of dishonesty for them might be trust, rather than honesty, as you might assume.

Note:

A person's core values are the things that are essential for them to have in their lives for them to be happy.

They are not something they aspire to or something they feel they *should* value. They are more than their preferred way of doing things, they are fundamental to the way they do things.

The coach needs to help the coachee to find their deepest layer of values.

Selecting the final Top 10:

Having asked all the above-mentioned questions, the coach will now have a long list of all the values that the coachee mentioned as being important to them.

The next step is to select the Top 10 core values.

Depending on how many have been elicited at this point, the coach could just show the coachee all the values noted and ask them simply to select their Top 10.

However, it may be necessary to coach them through this selection process. If there are several values that are quite similar e.g. honesty, openness, integrity, then ask the coachee:

'Which of those values resonates most with you?' 'Which is the stronger word?'

Help them to hone down the list, so it is more manageable to choose 10.

When some words are discounted, in favour of one core value, it is important to record the others too, this can be done in the 'Interpretation' column on the Values Summary. (See the example at the end of the Values Exploration section.) This ensures all of the important values are retained, however the core 10 are selected.

Examples of values identified:

Relationship values may include: honesty, connection, integrity, love, respect, support, appreciation, joy, kindness, duty, responsibility, tradition, loyalty, trust

Work values may include: achievement, success, fairness, respect, recognition, development, status, power, celebrity, knowledge, learning, innovation, making a difference, accountability, autonomy, flexibility

Fun and Leisure values may include creativity, sense of belonging/team, achievement, recognition, status, faith, caring, excitement, adventure

Environment values may include beauty, calmness, order, authenticity

Health values may include: wellbeing, energy, vitality

Money-related values may include: freedom, flexibility, choice, independence

Below are some examples of **Values identified from the negative emotion** question, i.e. the values missing when those emotions are felt, (with some examples of the behaviour causing the negative emotion in brackets):

- respect (positive opposite of disrespectful),
- fairness (positive opposite of unfairness, injustice),
- kindness (positive opposite of unkindness, cruelty, abuse, hurt),
- consideration (positive opposite of thoughtless, careless, inconsiderate),
- trust (positive opposite of betrayal, dishonesty),
- loyalty (positive opposite of disloyalty, unfaithfulness)

Coachees with low self-esteem

If you are working with a person with low self-esteem or someone who is very focused on what they do not want, rather than what they value in their lives, then you may need to ask these questions in a different way. They may find it easier to recall bad situations from the past and find the values that were missing rather than imagine a good time in the future and say what they would value.

Questions to ask include:

Relationships

'What was missing in your last relationship, that is important to you and that you would like to have in your next relationship?'

Work and career

'What was missing in your last job that is important to you and that you would like to have in your next role?'

Money and finance

'When you were faced with a time of financial hardship, what was missing that is important to you?'

Self development

'When you felt stuck and unable to move forward in your life, what was missing that is important to you?'

Health and fitness

'When you were feeling very stressed and not looking after yourself and your health, what was missing that is important to you?'

Environment

'Think of a time when you really hated your environment, at home or at work, what was missing that is important to you?'

Examples of possible scenarios:

If someone has been in a relationship where their partner was unfaithful to them, they may identify values of trust, honesty, loyalty and respect as things missing in that relationship that they would value in a future one.

In a job environment, they may identify a situation where they worked really hard but never got any thanks for what they did. Perhaps others got rewarded more for doing the same amount of work. Values of recognition and fairness may be important to them and were missing from that job environment.

Where there is stress, dissatisfaction, frustration and even anger in areas of our lives, then it is likely that something or someone is acting against our values. Alternatively, we ourselves may be dishonouring our own values. So it is helpful to identify what is missing in the situation to know what we want in a future one.

A word of warning: when identifying values, do not stop too soon.

Sometimes when asked what is important to them they say words like money, family and health, but these are 'chunk' words and not values, so do not accept them on the list.

As a coach, you need to take the coachee to a deeper level and ask, 'What does money give you?' e.g. security, independence, freedom, choice. Money is not the value but having some may give you more opportunity to live your life in line with your values.

Family is important to lots of people, but to find an individual's values you need to ask what they get from each relationship with their family members. It may be love, respect, connection, friendship, kindness, support, sense of purpose or many other different values. These are what you need to identify, so don't stop when someone says, 'Yes, family is very important to me'.

Values Exploration Technique 2: Values List

Overview:

This technique uses a pre-defined set of values (see the values list at the end of this technique) to choose from which makes it quicker than the questioning technique and aids comparison of words to help the coachee find the right one for them.

It involves less exploration at deep levels of feeling and so it is less likely that the coachee will become emotional in the session. It may be appropriate to use this method if time is limited or if the session is being held in the workplace. It is also useful if the coachee is finding it hard to identify values that are important to them.

Values Exploration using the questioning process in Technique 1 is likely to be more powerful than the Values List method. This is because it is possible to find words that are personalised and closer to an individual's values than the list may allow. The coach can take them to a deeper level of meaning to find their true core set of values. However choosing from the values list is still an effective way of identifying important values.

Inputs:

- The coach provides the values list

- The coachee knows what is important to them.

Outcomes:

- The coach works with the coachee to produce a set of 10 values that are core to what is important to the coachee

- This list of Top 10 values should give the coachee a feeling of 'me on a page' in that it will summarise the core of who they are, hence the term 'core values'

- The values from this technique will then be used in the prioritisation technique, to establish the order of their importance.

Timing:

This exploration can take up to 30 minutes and would be completed in the second coaching session. Allow the coachee time for reflection at the end to ensure they have chosen exactly the right words to represent what is important to them.

Tone:

The coach's tone is enquiring, encouraging and authoritative. The coachee will expect the coach to be knowledgeable on whether a word is a value or not, as they may want to choose a word that is not on the list but similar to something they see. They may also look to the coach to help them find the right word, so some encouraging input and options may be necessary.

Note:

Care must be taken to ensure the coachee selects values that are truly important to them and not those which they feel they should hold. There can be a tendency for people to choose values presented that they feel they ought to say are important, when actually this is more about morals than values or perhaps someone else's values that have been imposed on them. These should not be selected as they will not give the same degree of happiness and fulfilment when honoured, as a true value of the individual.

Values List

This table includes the top 120 values chosen during Values Exploration sessions, compiled from my experience of working with clients.

Additional values can be chosen provided they are values that are fundamental to the coachee's happiness and fulfilment.

Values List

stability	security	inner strength	joy	balance	moderation
happiness	fun/sense of humour	pleasure	relaxation	sense of belonging	inner peace
achievement	success	recognition	appreciation	ambition	being valued
passion	contentment	harmony	beauty	comfort	simplicity
honesty	truth	trust	openness	empathy	expression
equality	fairness	justice	courtesy	dignity	integrity
love	friendship	connection	kindness	companionship	camaraderie
freedom	choice	variety	abundance	adventure	excitement
faith	forgiveness	spirituality	tolerance	humility	grace
respect	consideration	loyalty	faithfulness	politeness	serenity
wisdom	intelligence	knowledge	insight	acceptance	honour
learning	development	growth	challenge	competition	excellence
sense of duty	tradition	order	sense of control	obedience	realism
authenticity	rationality	sense of authority	protection	compassion	patience
wellbeing	vitality	positivity	contribution	calmness	co-operation
community	cleanliness	decency	professionalism	competence	virtue/goodness
support	helpfulness	caring	service	generosity	nurturing
gratitude	determination	diligence/ hardworking	sense of purpose	making a difference	capability
innovation	creativity	resourcefulness	commitment	accountability	solitude
independence	responsibility	reliability	dependability	courage	quality

Technique Process

Individuals

Ask the coachee to review the list of values (see values list before the Technique Process) and identify initially which values resonate most with them, i.e. which are most important to them and which are the ones they can identify with most. Ideally they should list 15 or more values.

Questions to ask:

Coach:

'Which of these values are most important to you?'

'Which words resonate most with you?'

'Consider if that value was missing, how much would that matter?'

'Consider how fundamental each value is to your happiness and fulfilment'

*'If you feel you **ought** to choose a particular value, then disregard that one, it is not your core value, it will be one imposed upon you.'*

If they find that hard, you can ask them to focus on different aspects of their lives e.g. the ones from the Wheel of Life (used in Identifying Issues Technique 1).

Coach:

'When you think about your relationships with others, which of these values are most important?'

'Which of these values does having good health and fitness give you?'

'When you think about your work and career, which of these values need to be honoured for you to feel fulfilled and happy?'

'Which of these values does having money give you?'

When you think about your physical environment (at home and/or at work) which of these values are most important?'

'*Which of these values are honoured when you are having fun and leisure time, doing your hobbies, or developing yourself in some way?'*

Once the coachee has identified around 15 values, then ask them to select their core Top 10, i.e. the ten most important from the ones selected.

The coachee will end the session with a list of their individual core Top 10 Values, those that they feel represent what is important to them, that give them that 'me on a page' feeling. This forms the final list, which will then be prioritised.

Prioritising Values Technique 1: Visualisation & Comparison

Overview:

Whilst your values are and will always be important to you, the prioritisation you give them may vary over time and according to circumstance.

So whilst recognising that the prioritisation of values does change, it is useful to work out the priority each value has and then monitor this periodically and reflect on the changes.

Understanding the priority order helps to focus on the most important values first and also helps with decision-making, when honouring a higher priority value over another lower one may be necessary.

This technique uses a spoken visualisation process. It is more suited to people with a visual or auditory preference than a kinaesthetic preference. These people are more likely to favour the second prioritisation technique, using physical 'post-it' notes.

Inputs:

- The coach has the coachee's 10 chosen values noted down and the words of the visualisation technique to use in the session

- The coachee has an awareness of how important each value is to them.

Outcomes:

- A prioritised list of 10 values that are in order of importance to the coachee

- The prioritised values list from this technique will then be used in the measurement technique.

Timing:

This prioritisation usually takes around 10-15 minutes and would usually be completed towards the end of the second coaching session. If time does not allow, it can be completed at the next session. Allow the coachee time at the end of the technique to reflect on the order of priority they have given to their values.

Tone:

The coach's tone is neutral when giving the two values for comparison, it is essential not to lead the coachee to choose one value over another. The coach needs to be authoritative when setting the scene for the visualisation and may need to show some urgency in tone, to press the coachee for an immediate response to each question. Analysis and reflection are not required during this technique. This only happens once it is completed.

Technique Process:

- List the coachee's chosen 10 values down the left hand side of an A4 page, with space in between each one.

- The coach explains: *'Visualise yourself at a train station with two pieces of luggage in front of you, I will tell you the labels on each piece of luggage and you need to choose which piece of luggage you really want to have with you on your train journey. The train is about to leave so you will need to choose quickly. Feel free to close your eyes, if this helps you to concentrate.'*

- Then take the first value from the list of 10 and the second value and ask: *'One piece of luggage says (insert first value) the other piece of luggage says (insert second value) which do you really want to have with you on your journey?'*

- They can only choose one of the two words you read out and 'as the train is about to leave', you may need to press them for an answer, if they start to analyse it or think about it for more than a couple of seconds.

- Mark a 'I' tally to the right of the one they chose.

- Then read out the first and third value and ask them to choose, mark down their answer.

- Then read out the first and fourth value and so on, down the list.

- Once you have compared the first value with the other nine, tick off the first value on the left hand side of the page.

- Then read out the second and third value and follow the same process down the list, with the second and fourth, second and fifth and so on.

- Then repeat with the third and fourth, third and fifth etc.

- Once all of the values have been compared with each other, the coach says: *'Now open your eyes (if closed) and bring your awareness back into the room'.*

- Number the values in priority 1-10 (1 being highest and 10 being lowest). So the one with the highest tally that was chosen the most is the number one priority value at that point in time. The one with the lowest tally is the least important value in the list at this point in time, albeit still important.

- Re-write the list in that order, highest priority at the top.

- Ask the client to reflect on the priorities identified until they are happy with the order of importance.

- Transfer the list of values in priority order onto the Values Summary. (See template at the end of the Values Exploration section.)

- This prioritised list is then used for the Measuring Values Technique.

Prioritising Values Technique 2: 'Post-it' Method

Overview:

Whilst your values are and will always be important to you, the prioritisation you give them may vary over time and according to circumstance. So whilst recognising that the prioritisation of values does change, it is useful to work out the priority each value has and then monitor this periodically and reflect on the changes.

Understanding the priority order helps to focus on the most important values first and also helps with decision-making, when honouring a higher priority value over another lower one, may be necessary.

This prioritisation technique is usually quicker than the visualisation method. It is more suitable when working with a group, when individual questioning would not be appropriate or possible. It is also more suitable for people who may find the visualisation method challenging e.g. someone with a strong kinaesthetic preference, who prefers to use their sense of touch rather than their visual sense.

Inputs:

-   The coach has the coachee's 10 chosen values noted down and at least 10 'post-it' notes to use in the session

-   The coachee has an awareness of how important each value is to them.

Outcomes:

-   The coach works with the coachee to prioritise the set of 10 values that are core to what is important to the coachee

-   The prioritised list of values from this technique will then be used in the measurement technique.

Timing:

This prioritisation usually takes around 5-10 minutes and would usually be completed towards the end of the second coaching session. If time does not allow, it can be completed by the coachee after the session or at the next session.

Tone:

The coach's tone is supportive during this technique, however they should allow the coachee time and space to complete the technique themselves. Analysis and reflection may take place during this technique and once it is completed.

Technique Process:

- Ask the coachee to: *'Write each of their values on a separate small 'Post-it' note'*

- Then ask them to: *'Arrange the 'Post-it' notes vertically down an A4, or larger, sheet of paper and rearrange them into an order with the most important value at the top of the page to the least important at the bottom of the page.'*

- Once they are happy with the order of prioritisation, transfer the list of values in priority order onto the Values Summary. (See template at the end of the Values Exploration section.)

- This prioritised list is then used for the Measuring Values Technique.

Measuring Values Technique

Overview:

Once the coachee has a prioritised list of 10 core values, the final part of the Values Exploration process is to help them to measure how closely they are living their lives in line with their values and identify what improvements they would like to make.

This technique is a simple technique involving scoring each value from 0-10, then allocating a target score for any that are identified for improvement.

Inputs:

-   The coach has the coachee's prioritised Top 10 values noted down

-   The coachee has an awareness of how closely they are living their life in line with each value.

Outcomes:

-   Each of the coachee's Top 10 values is allocated a measure or score

-   A target score is allocated to those values the coachee wants to enhance in their lives; this is taken into the next step of the I-VALUE Coaching Framework.

Timing:

This measurement technique usually takes around 5-10 minutes and would usually be completed at the end of the second coaching session. If time does not allow, it can be completed by the coachee after the session or at the next session.

Tone:

The coach's tone is enquiring and supportive, as further realisation and self-awareness grows for the coachee.

Note:

Some coachees choose to target 3 or 4 values to enhance, whereas others may wish to improve them all e.g. to a 9 or 10. This is entirely the coachee's preference and no guidance is given by the coach in this process.

Technique Process:

In order to measure how closely the coachee is living their life in line with their values, follow these steps:

- Show the coachee their prioritised Top 10 list of values on the Values Summary, then ask them the following question for each value:

'On a scale of 0-10 how closely are you living your life in line with this value, with 0 being not at all and 10 being completely?'

- Note the number given in the right-hand column of the Values Summary against each value.

- For measurement purposes, it is useful to have a single score for each value to monitor changes over time. In the next step of the Framework there is a technique to analyse the score in more depth.

- Once each value has been given a measure or score, the next step is to identify any score that the coachee would like to increase. Ask:

'Which values would you like to focus on to increase your scores and what number would you like to increase each to?'

- They need to be specific about what number they want to increase each to and this is noted down to the right of the initial measure alongside the relevant value.

- This then gives a goal and a measure of success.

Example: Values Summary

Priority Number	Core Value	Interpretation	Score and Target Score
1-10	*What's important to you? Enter core values here:*	*What does that mean to you? What does that give you?*	*How are you living your life in line with your values? Score 0-10 → Target Score*
1	Happiness	Enjoyment, pleasure, excitement, variety, sense of humour	6 → 10
=1*	Being Valued	Acceptance, inner strength, courage, commitment	5 → 8
3	Wellbeing	Energy, feeling good, relaxation, development, improvement	6 → 9
=3*	Trust	Loyalty	5 → 10
=3*	Honesty	Openness, loyalty	5 → 9
6	Friendship	Understanding, connection, support, kindness, sharing, familiarity	7 → 9
7	Love	Closeness, connection, support, kindness, caring	6 → 10
8	Stability	Security, balance, consistency, sense of control, commitment, discipline, routine	5 → 10
9	Recognition	Appreciation, external validation, achievement	5 → 7
10	Respect	Fairness, consideration, moderation, professionalism	6 → 8

* = is used when the prioritisation of one or more values is the same

(e) any ... ation of the ve...
    the v...

28.5 The ending of ...ract does not affect the ...y of the offen...
    default.

THE SELLER
_____

THE PURCHASER
_____

WITNESSES
_____

Security

A   Awareness of Self and Change Needed

Having completed the Values Exploration, a time of reflection is needed to help the coachee to use the new knowledge that they have gained of their core values. This step helps to raise their self-awareness and will support them in identifying the changes they need to make in their lives to align to their values.

If time is not taken to do this, then an opportunity for the coachee to affirm their identity, by connecting with themselves in the past and the present, is missed. They may not learn the lessons of their past and may not know themselves so well in the present.

The 'A' step in the I-VALUE Coaching Framework is for Awareness of Self and Change Needed.

Identifying their core values in the previous step of the coaching process gives a person an amazing sense of clarity of who they are and what is important to them. It is that 'Me on a Page' moment that I hear from many clients, when they reflect on their Values Summary and what it means to them.

In this step, they raise their self-awareness. They gain a better understanding of why they experienced certain emotions in the past, why they reacted the way they did, why they made the choices they made and why it felt the way it did.

The coachee will learn to understand their emotions, reactions and choices and so they will start to understand themselves and how they interact with others better.

It is key, at this point, to reiterate to the coachee that, by honouring the core values in their Summary in all aspects of their life, language, behaviour, choices and actions, they will feel a sense of happiness, fulfilment and many other positive emotions.

This is the point, I call the 'Values Glow', the wonderful feeling you get when you or someone else is honouring your values. I use the word 'glow' because some people actually blush when they feel their values are being met.

The more core values the coachee honours, the stronger the positive emotion they will feel. Also the higher the priority of those values the stronger the emotion too.

Equally, whenever the coachee dishonours their values in any aspect of their life, they will feel a negative emotion e.g. anger, sadness, frustration. Again the more values dishonoured and the higher the priority of those values, the stronger the negative emotion they will feel.

The learning really starts when the coachee begins to understand their values and has more awareness of what their values mean in their lives.

It is often when people have their 'lightbulb moment' of realisation, when things start to make sense, that they really start to understand who they are, why they are the way they are and what makes them tick. They can gain a great sense of clarity.

In this step, there is also an opportunity to review the issues identified in the first Issue Identification step of the I-VALUE Coaching Framework, in the knowledge of their values. This raises awareness of the reasons for and causes of the problems they are experiencing and allows further exploration in a values-led approach.

At this point, the focus can be on one specific issue which may affect several values or on one value that is affected by many aspects of a person's life.

Alternatively, a full review of all aspects of life may be appropriate, to establish all the areas that are having a negative impact on their values and in which they want to make some change.

The coachee can look at whether they are honouring their own values. They might explore who in their lives is 'stomping all over' or dishonouring their values and who is honouring them, and what they want to change. This leads on to the next step in the Framework, in which they learn techniques to help them live their lives more closely aligned to their core values.

This step may happen at the end of the second session, directly following the Values Exploration process, or it may be a separate session on its own, depending on how long the elicitation takes, how quickly the coachee grasps the concept and how much change is needed.

The coachee can also be encouraged to take time to reflect on their values in between coaching sessions.

What new level of self-awareness are the people you coach missing out on, by not taking the time to reflect on their values?

'Your vision will become clear only when you can look into your own heart. Who looks outside, dreams; who looks inside, awakens.' C.G. Jung

Awareness of Self in the Past

As the coachee's self-awareness grows, it may be useful for them to review decisions, events, reactions etc. from their past, in light of their values. This will help them to understand the emotions they felt and why they responded the way they did. This helps to embed the process of using their Values Summary to help them understand how they feel.

Awareness Technique 1: Positive/Negative Emotion

Positive Emotion

- Ask the coachee to recall a situation when they felt strong positive emotion. (They do not need to give you all the detail of the situation.) As they recall it, you may see a smile, a 'happy tear', or a slight blush – the 'Values Glow'.

- Then ask them to look down their Values Summary and state which values were being honoured by what was happening, at that moment in time.

- Give them time to reflect and become aware that they felt those emotions because those values were being honoured.

For example: in a workplace situation when someone receives an award for something they have worked hard for and that matters to them, they will feel a real 'Values Glow' if they have strong values of achievement, success, recognition and respect.

Negative Emotion

- This time, ask the coachee to recall a situation when they felt a strong negative emotion. (They do not need to give you all the detail of the situation.) As they recall it, you may see some of the anger, frustration or sadness in their eyes or through their body language or the tone of their voice.

- Again ask them to look down their Values Summary and state which values were being dishonoured by what was happening, at that moment in time.

- Give them time to reflect and become aware that they felt those emotions because those values were being dishonoured.

For example, if someone has a strong value of 'making a difference' or 'contribution' and they are out of work, they may well feel a sense of sadness or frustration. This is because those values are not being honoured at that moment in time. Just understanding where that emotion is coming from allows them to take a look at their life and seek out opportunities to make a difference and contribute to the world in some way; e.g. through volunteering. This will immediately give them more of a sense of fulfilment.

Awareness of Self in the Present

When people are beginning to understand their values, they often ask whether it is how they behave that honours their values of whether it is how others behave to them. The answer to that is both, along with how we behave to ourselves.

I came across this model some years ago as a very simple way of explaining the complexity of values. A basic triangle, with the value at the centre and one side of the triangle representing 'Me to Others', another side representing 'Others to Me' and the base side representing 'Me to Me'. Simply it states that all three sides of the triangle need to be honoured to feel a sense of balance, harmony and happiness, in respect of that value.

The sides of the triangle represent the various aspects of behaviour, so how we behave to others, how they behave to us and most fundamentally, how we treat ourselves, in respect of that value.

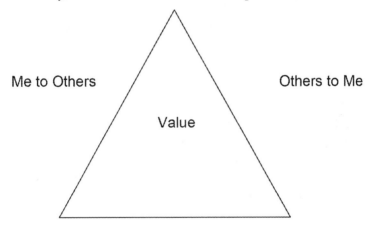

Me to Others

Others to Me

Value

Me to Me

The 'Values Triangle'

For example, if we take the value of love, for this value to be truly honoured, we need to show love to others, be loved by others and love ourselves. In the Values Exploration step of the I-VALUE Coaching

Framework, it describes the method of measuring where you are right now in terms of honouring a value by giving a 'gut feel' score from 0-10 for how closely you are living your life in line with that value, with 0 being not at all and 10 being completely.

For many values, it is helpful to break that score down by scoring each side of the Values Triangle to help to identify aspects that need adjustment.

So for measurement purposes, it is useful to have a single score for each value to monitor changes over time. For action purposes, it is even more useful to break that score down to the three aspects, so the coachee can really see where the changes are needed for them to feel happier and more fulfilled.

For example, the coachee might give a score of 6 out of 10, for how closely they are living their life in line with their value of love. Then, by breaking that overall score down, by scoring each of the three sides, it gives a better understanding of what is going on.

Value: Love:	Overall satisfaction:	6
	Me to Others:	8
	Me to Me:	6
	Others to Me:	4

They might score 'Me to Others' as an 8 out of 10, as they feel they are showing love to others in their life. They might score 'Me to Me' as a 6 as they feel ok about themselves, but there's room for improvement. They might score 'Others to Me' as a 4, as they feel that important people in their life are not showing them the love they want, need or deserve.

In this case a first step might be to focus on enhancing the Me to Me score, as the more we honour a value in the way we behave to ourselves the easier it is for others to change their behaviour towards us.

In my work with clients, I have noticed a number of trends. When clients are unhappy in a work situation or a relationship, often this corresponds with low scores on the 'Others to Me' side of their Values Triangle. When they are generally feeling unfulfilled, it is the 'Me to Others' side that is not being honoured.

Clients with a low self-esteem tend to have very low 'Me to Me' scores for key values such as love, trust, honesty, respect, as they do not value themselves sufficiently to show these behaviours to themselves. The 'Others to Me' score is correspondingly low too, as they may not be allowing others to show them these values either.

Once you have identified your values, seeing how closely you are living your life in line with those values is always an amazing step in raising your self-awareness. The key is then what you do with that new knowledge to improve your life.

All aspects of the coachee's life and all three sides of the value (Me to Me, Me to Others and Others to Me) can be taken into account in this exercise, so they can identify specific areas of their life or relationship with themselves and others, in which their values are not in alignment.

The exercise is non-judgmental, it is not about beating oneself up for past behaviours; it is only about identifying areas for development.

When considering all three sides to each value, if the measure is significantly different on each side, note down each score and this will help to focus attention in the most appropriate areas to see where changes are most needed.

Awareness Technique 2: Aspects of Values

Overview:

To enhance the coachee's self-awareness and to identify specific areas for change, this technique is a simple method to break down each score into three constituent parts.

This works particularly well for what I call 'Values for the Journey' e.g. love, respect, honesty, kindness. These are values that are shown every day in our interactions with others and demonstrated in how we treat ourselves.

This technique is less appropriate for what I call 'Outcome Values' e.g. success, sense of purpose, independence. These are values that one aims to attain in life and are less relevant to how people interact with each other day to day.

Inputs:

- The coach has the coachee's completed Values Summary

- The coachee has an awareness of how much they demonstrate those values to themselves and in their interactions with others and how much others display those values to them.

Outcomes:

- A measure or score is allocated to all three aspects of each chosen value

- At the end of the technique the coachee will have identified particular aspects, for each chosen value that need addressing. These are taken into the next step of the I-VALUE Framework.

Timing:

This measurement technique usually takes around 5-10 minutes and could be completed at the end of the second coaching session. If time does not allow, it can be completed by the coachee after the session or at the next session.

Tone:

The coach's tone is enquiring and supportive, as further realisation and self-awareness grows for the coachee. The coach needs to be knowledgeable on which values are appropriate for this technique, i.e. which are 'Values for the Journey'.

Note:

Some coachees choose just one value to focus on, whereas others may wish to focus on several. This is entirely the coachee's preference and no guidance is given by the coach in this process.

Technique Process:

In order to measure how closely the coachee is living their life in line with each aspect of appropriate 'Values for the Journey', follow these steps:

- Show the coachee their prioritised and measured Top 10 Values Summary. Then assist them in selecting appropriate values for further detailed measurement.

- Then for each value chosen, the coach asks them to score each aspect:

    - *'For the aspect of 'Me to Others', on a scale of 0-10 how much are you showing this value in your interactions with others?'*

    - *'For the aspect of 'Others to Me', on a scale of 0-10 how much are others showing this value to you, in your interactions with them?'*

    - *'For the aspect of 'Me to Me', on a scale of 0-10 how much are you showing this value in your treatment of yourself?'*

- Note the number given in the right-hand column of the Values Summary against each aspect of each value.

- Once the aspects of appropriate values have been given a measure or score, the next step is to identify any that the coachee would like to increase, the coach asks:

    - *'Which scores would you like to increase and to what number would you like to increase each one?'*

- They need to be specific about what number they want to increase each to and the coach notes this down to the right of the initial measure alongside the relevant value, in the right hand column of the Values Summary.

- This then gives a goal and a measure of success.

Example Values Summary with Aspects Scores

Number	Value	Interpretation	Score
1-10	*What's important to you? Enter core values here:*	*What does that mean to you? What does that give you?*	*How are you living your life in line with your values? – Score 0-10 →* Target Score
3	Trust	Loyalty	6 → 10 Me to me 4 → 10 Me to others 5 → 10 Others to me 7 → 10
=3*	Honesty	Openness, integrity	5 → 9 Me to me 5 → 9 Me to others 7 → 9 Others to me 5 → 9
6	Friendship	Understanding, connection, support, kindness, sharing, familiarity	7 → 9 Me to me 5 → 9 Me to others 7 → 9 Others to me 6 → 9
7	Love	Closeness, connection, support, kindness, caring	6 → 10 Me to me 4 → 10 Me to others 8 → 10 Others to me 6 → 10
10	Respect	Fairness, consideration, moderation, professionalism	6 → 8 Me to me 5 → 8 Me to others 7 → 8 Others to me 5 → 8

* = is used when the prioritisation of one or more values is the same

Awareness of Changes Needed

The final part of the Awareness step in the I-VALUE Coaching Framework is to bring together all the information gathered from the first three steps of the Framework:

Issue Identification:

- The Wheel of Life current scores, target scores and noted issues.
- Any issues, or areas to focus on, identified from the Questioning Technique.

Values Exploration:

- The Values Summary current and target scores for values to focus on.

Awareness of Self and Change Needed:

- The aspects of values current and target scores for values to focus on.
- Any issues arising from the Awareness step in the framework.

With the coachee, the coach summarises all the information and identifies common areas for change, specific issues to focus on, and particular values or aspects of values that need addressing.

There may be one theme that runs through the coaching sessions so far or there may be several. If there are several, the coach can ask the coachee to prioritise the order in which the issues are addressed in future sessions.

e.g. Wheel of Life aspects: work first, then relationships, then family
e.g. Values: balance first, then wellbeing, then trust.
e.g. Issues: no work/life balance first, then relationship not moving forward, then difficulties within the family.

The information from this review can be captured on the Awareness Summary template below. This can be used in future sessions to focus on priority areas where change is needed and the priority values chosen for enhancement.

Awareness Summary

Wheel of Life Aspects to enhance:	Values to enhance:	Problems/Issues/ Challenges to resolve:
•	•	•
•	•	•
•	•	•
•	•	•
•	•	•

Belonging

L   Living a Values-Led Life

This step includes a range of techniques that can be used to support the coachee in making the changes needed in their lives to align their thoughts, language, behaviour, decisions and actions, more closely to their values. This is where the change begins to start living a values-led life.

As a coach, you may be familiar with some of the techniques included here, however as you will see, the difference is that they have been enhanced to take a values approach. Without that enhancement, the techniques may help the coachee to make changes in their lives, but will they be the right changes? Will those changes take them on the best path for their lives or will they have to change things again when they do not find fulfilment?

The 'L' step in the I-VALUE Coaching Framework is for Living a Values-Led Life.

In Part 1, it was established that living your life in alignment with your own core values leads to increased happiness, fulfilment and satisfaction.

The first three steps of the I-VALUE Coaching Framework focus on how to identify the issues a coachee is facing and how to elicit their core values and use them to build their self-awareness.

This part of the Framework focuses on helping the coachee to live their life according to their values. It includes a range of applications that offer values-based techniques to support many aspects of change that a person may want and need to make.

Using these techniques supports the coachee in aligning their thoughts, their communication and their behaviours to their core values and thus beginning to live a values-led life.

Lindsay West

Applications include:

Goal-setting with Values

- Designing your ideal life
- GROW with Values model

Managing Emotions with Values

- Motivation
- Confidence and self-esteem
- Reducing stress

Making Change with Values

- Decision-making and prioritising
- Problem-solving
- Action planning

At the end of this step in the process, the coachee will have experienced and applied several techniques to begin the change to living a values-led life. The techniques used in the coaching sessions then can be applied by the coachee in their daily life, within an appropriate agreed timescale.

This part of the Framework may take place over three or more sessions, depending on the level of change an individual wants to make. Additional sessions can be arranged to focus on a specific technique to address a specific issue e.g. time management.

How closely are your coachees living their lives in line with their values?

**Understanding your values gives clarity,
living your values brings happiness.**

Goal-Setting with Values

The coachee's core values have been established and they have used them to help grow their self-awareness. The next step in the coaching process is to help the coachee to work out what living a values-based life and career means for them. It includes planning action to make it happen. This starts with goal-setting, which is the first section of the 'L' step: Living a Values-Led Life, in the I-VALUE Coaching Framework.

The benefits of goal-setting come from having an increased sense of purpose and direction, knowing how to move forward, make progress and take action to live a values-based life.

Two techniques are described here:

- The first, Ideal Life, is a comprehensive method for goal-setting incorporating a 'whole life' view, using all of the individual's core values to describe their ideal life. This takes place in the third coaching session of the programme and takes approximately 60 minutes.
- The second technique is GROW with Values and is based on the widely recognised GROW model (GROW stands for Goal, Reality, Options and Way Forward). In this technique one value is selected as the goal. This is a quicker technique to complete, it takes about 30 minutes. It focuses attention on making change to enhance one specific value. This can be used in any coaching session.

The Ideal Life method for goal-setting and planning is a values-based visualisation technique, which involves the coachee imagining their ideal life in three years time, when all their core values are being met. A three-year timescale is used, as it is far enough away for anything to change but not too far that it's hard to imagine.

The technique incorporates the use of all five senses to get as real a picture as possible and then it uses a backward timeline to aid planning of actions from the third year back to the present.

Traditionally, with goal-setting, most people and indeed most coaches select an area of life in which to set a goal e.g. career. Goals are usually focused around achieving, having or doing something either work or life related e.g. getting a new job. This can be a beneficial method, if by chance the goal selected honours a person's values.

Making 'living their values' the goal, however, has more motivation attached because these are the things that are important to the coachee. It also brings more satisfaction, once it is achieved, as their values are the things that will make them happy and feel fulfilled, so it is a perfect approach for goal-setting.

The GROW with Values technique is useful for focusing on a goal of enhancing one specific value, then identifying options and agreeing actions to take forward.

The traditional GROW model focuses on a particular goal e.g. getting a new job; whereas the Values approach would focus on doing the things needed to enhance a value e.g. Achievement.

In this way, whether the actions planned are big or small, they will enhance that value and you will feel better as a result. Getting a new job may or may not make you feel better depending on whether, by chance, your values happen to be enhanced in the role and environment you choose or not.

So rather than taking that chance, using a values-based approach to goal-setting gives more certainty and faster results.

Goal-Setting Technique 1: Ideal Life

Overview:

This goal-setting technique uses visualisation to help the coachee build a detailed picture of their Ideal Life in the future, as if it were happening now. They imagine what it would be like if they were living their life in line with their values. This includes honouring their values to themselves and to others and having others honour their values too.

By asking the coachee to visualise this, you take them forward in time and they imagine that this goal has already been achieved. In this way the goal becomes the outcome. By coaching them to examine what is happening, who is present, what people are saying and how they feel, it becomes more real. It develops a strong image for them to remember and they start to feel what it is like to be happy and fulfilled.

The technique also uses a timeline process which is helpful in producing a timed plan to achieve the Ideal Life. Having identified what is happening in three years' time, you then talk the coachee back to the present day, noting what needs to be in place in two years, one year, six months, three months and what needs to be different today for the three-year plan to be possible. Using the timeline, they learn more about what is needed to achieve that outcome and develop manageable steps to get there.

This method helps to remove any fear and improves their chances of success. It is also very helpful for those who find it hard to take the first step. Once they know what is ahead, it makes it much easier and less stressful.

Inputs:
- The coach has the coachee's Values Summary and note paper, as they will be recording everything the coachee says to produce a typed plan for them

- The coachee brings their understanding of what it would be like to live a values-led life and have all their values honoured every day.

Outcomes:

- Clear definition of what a values-led life means for the coachee

- A detailed plan of the actions needed and the changes to be made, over the next three years, to achieve that outcome

- Improved sense of purpose and direction in life.

Timing: This technique would be completed in one coaching session of approximately 60 minutes, usually the third one of the programme.

Note: It is important to record the coachee's actual words in this session so a typed-up full plan can be given to the coachee. They will need this to refer to the agreed actions and to keep them on track towards achieving their goal and Ideal Life outcome. It is helpful if it is written in their own words, with no additional interpretation from the coach. The coachee can add/amend/delete anything they want to afterwards, as it is their plan and flexibility should be encouraged. Recording the session, with permission, is another option as opposed to note-taking to get an accurate record.

Technique Process:

Visualisation:

The coach starts by introducing the Ideal Life technique and the process to be used in the session (use the explanation in the Introduction and Overview above). The coachee can have their eyes closed for the visualisation, if they find it helpful.

The Coach asks the coachee the following questions and notes down the answers. The coachee needs to describe everything in the present tense as if they are there right now, ask them to do so if they start to talk in the future tense. Also ensure the coachee is stating everything in the positive, what is happening, rather than what is not happening. Ask them to do this if negative statements are heard at any point.

Coach:

'Imagine your Ideal Life in three years' time. That's far enough away for anything to change and not so far that you can't imagine it. All your values are being honoured by you and those around you, tell me what is happening?'

'What can you see around you? Who is there?'

'What can you hear around you? What are people saying?'

'What does it feel like? What can you touch around you?'

'What tastes and smells are there?'

'Think about each of your values, how are they evident in your life?'

Note: Ask them all the questions to get them to try out each of their senses. They may not have an answer for some of them and that is fine, people have different preferences for the senses they use. It is important to keep them focused on their values and what it means for those values to be honoured in their lives.

Once a really clear picture of their Ideal Life is described, you may start to see the 'Values Glow' in them as they connect to a time when all their values are honoured and a physical response is visible from the emotion they feel.

Timeline:

The next part of the process is to work backwards from the 3-year outcome to the present day, to do this the coach ask:

'What needs to be in place in 2 years' time for the 3-year outcome to be possible'

'What needs to be in place in 1 year for the 2-year plan to be possible?'

'What needs to be in place in 6 months' time for the 1-year plan to be possible?'

'What changes need to be made now for the 6 month plan to be possible?'

Once the coach has worked through each of these questions with the coachee, they will have a clear plan of action to take them forward to achieving their Ideal Life outcome in three years' time.

At the end, double-check with the coachee that the actions agreed do continue to honour all their values. If any action planned has a negative impact on any of the coachee's values, then ask them to adjust that action.

It is important that each step honours their values; it may leave one or two neutral, but must not have a negative impact.

The coach then types it up and sends it to the client, who needs to note actions in their diary and start to make the agreed changes in their lives.

At each future coaching session, it is useful to refer back to this plan and review progress made with the coachee.

Goal-Setting Technique 2: GROW with Values

Overview:

The 'GROW' model is a widely used coaching framework. It provides a good structure for a coaching session. It is focused on establishing a **G**oal, looking at the **R**eality of what is happening now and what is stopping progress, then identifying **O**ptions available and agreeing a **W**ay forward to progress towards achieving the Goal.

The values-based version of the GROW model is simply to make 'enhancing a core value' the goal and follow the same process.

When the coachee completed their values elicitation (in the Values Exploration step of the I-VALUE Coaching Framework), they measured how closely they were living their life in line with their values. They marked some as an area for improvement, with a score out of 10 that they wanted to achieve, so they could select one of these as the goal to use in this technique.

They may also have further awareness (from the Awareness step in the Framework) of the issues in respect of this value from exploring the different aspects: Me to Others, Others to Me, Me to Me. It is also likely that there will be links back to the Wheel of Life scores and other issues (identified in the Issue Identification step of the Framework).

This technique draws all these together to form a clear way forward. The results of values-based goal-setting and planning are instant. The clarity alone leads to an increase in the sense of fulfilment, even relief that finally, there is an understanding of what was wrong, why and what needs to be done about it.

Inputs:

- The coach brings the GROW with Values model and relevant questions

- The coachee chooses the core value that they would like to enhance.

Outcomes:

- A structured analysis leading to a set of planned actions to achieve the goal of enhancing a value

- Increased motivation for change.

Timing:

This technique takes between 30-60 minutes and can be used in any coaching session to focus on one value, when appropriate.

Notes:

The Way Forward output needs to be typed up for the coachee to start working on the agreed actions and they need to enter the timescales into their diary/schedule.

Technique Process:

Goal

Gain clarity on the Goal by asking:

'Which of your core values would you like to enhance in your life?'

'What is important to you about achieving this?'

If you like SMART goals, ask yourself:

'What would honouring this value look, sound and feel like?' Be specific.

'How will you know you have achieved this?' Make it measurable.

'When do you want it to happen?' Allocate a timescale.

Reality

Establish the current position, the reality, by asking:

'How closely are you living your life in line with this value now?

'What scores out of 10 do you give for each aspect: Me to Others, Others to Me, Me to Me?'

'What have you done so far towards this goal?'

'What is stopping you making progress?'

Options

Explore the options for change, by asking:

'What could you do differently to enhance how you live your life in line with that value?'

Other ways of asking this question are:

'Let your mind run free. What could you do to move you forward?'

'What options do you have to enhance those scores in each aspect of this value?'

'If you are living your life in line with this value, what is different from how it has been in the past?'

List as many options as possible.

Way Forward

Choose one option to turn into an action plan towards achieving your goal and enhancing your chosen value.

List the actions to be taken and reflect on them.

Questions to ask to encourage clarity for an action plan are:

'What will you do?'

'What might stop you?'

'What will you do to make sure it doesn't?'

'Who else is involved?'

'When will you tell them?'

'When will you actually take that first step?'

At this point, it is important to check that the plans decided upon honour the other values held. **If any plans dishonour another value, then the plan needs to be adjusted, to at least leave that value neutral** (i.e. neither honour or dishonour that value). Additionally, if increased **motivation is needed, draw on other specific values to support achieving the plan.**

GROW with Values Template

Goal: *Enter the value to be enhanced:*

Reality: *Describe the current reality in respect of living life in line with this value:*

Overall score out of 10:
Score out of 10 for Me to Others aspect:
Score out of 10 for Others to Me aspect:
Score out of 10 for Me to Me aspect:

Options: *What options do you have to enhance this value?*
List every idea you have:

-
-
-
-
-
-
-
-
-
-

Way Forward: *Which options do you choose to make progress in enhancing this value in your life? Decide on the action you will take and when:*

Action: Start: Complete:

-
-
-
-
-

Managing Emotions with Values

The second section of the 'L' step: Living a Values-Led Life in the I-VALUE Coaching Framework is about learning how to use values to manage emotions. This includes:

- Enhancing motivation
- Improving confidence and self-esteem
- Reducing stress

In Part 1, it was established that values and emotions are strongly connected. A positive emotion will be felt when our values are honoured and a negative emotion will be felt when they are dishonoured.

The more of our core values affected, the stronger the emotion will be. Also the higher the level of importance or priority the person gives to those values, the stronger the emotion will be.

Once we understand our values, we start to understand our emotions and where they come from. Values are the core of who we are. They are the essence of what is important to us and, as such, they are our key motivators.

So we can draw on our values to motivate us to take action to attain the things we aim for in life and thus enhance our sense of happiness and feelings of fulfilment.

The opposite applies too, so if our values are being dishonoured then this will have a de-motivating affect.

The more we are living our lives in line with our values, the more confidence we have and the higher our self esteem will be.

If we use our values to guide us in our journey through life, it helps to reduce the stress of difficult decisions and challenging situations.

The techniques described here can also help with:

- Improving the impression we make and our impact e.g. at social events, networking events or important meetings
- Controlling nerves e.g. for job interviews, first dates, presentations, performances
- Improving personal effectiveness e.g. for managing a stressful or challenging situation, or dealing with a potential conflict.

Managing Emotions: Enhancing Motivation

Motivation is the force that initiates, guides and maintains goal-oriented behaviour. It is what causes us to take action. When motivation is lacking we can become 'stuck' and unable to move forward with our goals.

It is often the trigger for people to seek the help of a coach, as they feel unable to help themselves to get out of the situation in which they find themselves.

Values motivate us, they are what drive us, so by 'tapping in' to our individual values, we can draw on the strength they give us to motivate us to achieve whatever we want to achieve.

By first understanding our core values then by drawing on them, we can ensure we are motivated to be who we want to be, do what we want to do and have what we want to have in our lives and careers.

If our values are not being honoured by our own behaviour or by that of those around us, not only will we become unhappy, but it is likely we will become de-motivated too.

For example, people who work in an environment where their values are not honoured, or worse are actually being dishonoured, often become so de-motivated, they find it hard to take action to get themselves out of the job and into one they enjoy. Equally, people who work in an environment where their values are being honoured will thrive and be very motivated to achieve their goals and will perform at a high level.

There are many situations in life and work when we need additional motivation to get through something that is challenging to us, so learning how to access our inner motivational resources, in the moment we need them, can be extremely beneficial.

The following technique draws on the 'States' technique from Neuro-Linguistic Programming (NLP). However, rather than choosing to access a random state, our focus here is to access specific core values, as these are our biggest motivators.

Managing Emotions Technique 1: Values States for Motivation

Overview:

This technique helps the coachee to access or 'tap into' their inner resources to motivate them to do what they need to do. This is made more effective by asking them to choose one of their own values that would be a useful, resourceful state. Some examples might be openness, respect, adventure, caring.

Accessing their inner resources helps to enhance their motivation to take action, face challenges or make changes. Using one of their own core values to do this makes it even more powerful. This technique draws on a natural state of the coachee as values are their natural motivators.

Often it is the very value that is missing in a situation that they need to access and draw on to motivate them to make change. Sometimes drawing on other core values is helpful to strengthen that motivation.

Inputs:

- The coach has the coachee's Values Summary

- The coachee has awareness of a situation that they are struggling to improve or make changes with, that they are stuck in or are de-motivated about.

Outcomes:

- The coachee gains motivation which leads to them taking action to achieve goals and attain the things they aim for in life

- This realises their potential and enhances their sense of happiness and feelings of fulfilment.

Timing:

This technique is very flexible and can be completed in 10-30 minutes, depending on how much detail the client needs to include.

Tone:

The coach's tone is supportive, as the client may be emotional and the coach also needs to be encouraging and curious, to help the coachee through the process.

Note:

Emotion shown by the client is helpful as this means they are working with the right value and that this is a strong value that is important to them.

Technique Process:

1. Identify the negative emotion, leading to the de-motivated state. This may have been identified in the first coaching session in the Issue Identification step of the Framework and it is now time to address it.

   Example: a single person who feels bored on their own and complains that they never have any fun but they are too de-motivated to put the effort into going onto dating websites or socialising. They have given a score of 0 for Relationship and 2 for Fun and Leisure on their Wheel of Life. They have core values that include: love, fun, achievement and adventure

2. Identify the core value that is not being honoured in this situation.

   Example response: It's too much like hard work, it's no fun, yes fun is the value.

3. Ask the coachee to focus on that value and imagine that it is being honoured in that situation and get them to notice the differences.

   Example response: If it was fun then I would be having a laugh, picking people online for me to date with the help of my friends, I would be going out every week meeting different people, going to new places. I would be enjoying dating and wouldn't want to be sitting at home and watching TV.

4. Now ask the coachee what actions they can take to enhance that value in this aspect of their lives.

   Example response: I can invite my friends over for a date-choosing night and they can help me choose some guys to email from the dating websites. I can make my profile more fun and look for guys with the same value. When I go on dates I can try out some new bars and restaurants. I can chill out about the whole thing and start enjoying myself and have some fun finding the right man for me.

5. Ask the coachee which other values they could draw on to enhance their motivation even more.

    Example response: I could make it more of an adventure, rather than thinking of the effort I'm having to put in. I can remember that love is the outcome I'm seeking. That helps to get me in the right mood. I can see each date I have as an achievement, even if I decide not to see them again.

6. Ask how they feel about the situation now and when they will start to take action.

    Example response: I'm already looking forward to getting started. I'm going to get the girls round on Saturday night, although I might have a look through a few profiles tonight. I don't want them choosing someone awful! Yes I'm really ready to have some fun. Thank you so much!

Managing Emotions: Enhancing Motivation

Case Study – Kali

Kali came to me looking for clarity and direction in her life. She described problems in her relationship and other problems with some friends and also with some work colleagues.

She felt unloved, let down, lonely, helpless and sad. We had established her core values in a previous session. When, in this particular session, she became extremely emotional, I asked her to look at her values and tell me which one was particularly missing in her life at that moment. She quickly replied 'sense of belonging'.

Rather than spend the rest of our time in the coaching session analysing why she felt like that, why she was crying, who had taken that away from her or what had happened, I simply asked her to focus on that value of 'sense of belonging'. I asked her to imagine it was being honoured in her life and what the differences were and then I asked her what she could do to enhance that value of 'sense of belonging'.

She easily listed five specific, timed actions she could take over the next week that would directly enhance that value.

By the second action, she had recovered herself and was no longer crying. By the third action, she was really focused and thinking hard. By the fourth action, she was relaxing and completely calm. By the time she came up with the fifth action, she had visibly grown in confidence and motivation to make some changes. She was laughing and smiling and feeling really happy.

This took around ten minutes and just by identifying and focusing on one value, she transformed into a happy, confident and self-assured young woman.

By focusing on what you can do to enhance a particular value, it immediately has the effect of enhancing it. Just by focusing on something important to you, your motivation grows and grows.

Ten minutes from sobbing tears to beaming smiles, just by focusing on one value – it's powerful stuff.

Managing Emotions: Increasing Confidence & Self-Esteem

Confidence and self-esteem are states of mind and being. They are attitudes based on the perception we have of ourselves. They can be consciously improved, using values to access inner resources and practise new attitudes, behaviours and language.

For many people, having low levels of confidence and self-esteem, can seriously hold them back and stop them from achieving what they want in life. It may have been an issue for them for much of their lives. It is often a reason that people turn to coaches for help.

Increased inner strength, motivation and a sense of empowerment can be gained through using values, resulting in realised potential and improved effectiveness.

Using the following technique helps the coachee to build confidence and self-esteem through values-based focus, thoughts, behaviour and language. By repeatedly practising this technique, their inner confidence and self-esteem grow and grow. This helps them to create a better impression and have a more powerful impact on others, in any social or work situation. It can be used for anything from a first date to a job interview.

This technique aims to channel potential through building and showing confidence via the way they look, how they think, how they behave and the language they use.

By making changes to their own posture, movement, gestures, eye contact, behaviour etc. in different situations, they will feel good and create a better impression with those around them, thus 'looking and feeling the part'.

It is more effective than just acting, because it is based on the coachee's own values and therefore it is tapping in to who they really are and their inner motivation, so it adds authenticity.

Language is important here too, as it is:

- the interpretation we give our experiences
- the externalisation of our perception and values

- the impression we create
- the meaning we give something
- the meaning other people receive from us

Language is a good indicator of whether the coachee is living their values in every day life at home and work. Often they can use better, more powerful language to show what is really important to them.

It is helpful for the coachee to reflect on how the language they use every day affects how people view them and how they feel about themselves. If they are using negative language this reinforces a negative state in the subconscious and this leads to feeling even worse in themselves. Additionally, people may view them as a negative person, lacking in self-esteem and confidence.

Values-based words motivate us and increase our self-esteem and confidence. A small change to the words used can be very empowering, so it is important for the coachee to take care with the language they use.

This technique uses powerful values-driven language and can have a positive impact in any situation, as the coachee will feel more confident and better about themselves.

It includes use of affirmations. These are positive motivational statements that are personal and stated in the present tense. To be effective they require repetition many times, on a daily basis, to continue to reinforce the improved levels of confidence and self-esteem.

'By repeating an affirmation over and over again, it becomes embedded in the subconscious mind and eventually becomes your reality. That is why you need to be careful what you think and believe, because that is exactly what you will get!'

Anthony Robbins, coach and motivational speaker[*]

---

[*] See reference 6

Managing Emotions Technique 2: Increasing Confidence & Self- Esteem

Overview:

This technique allows the coachee to influence the impression they create by accessing their inner resources, drawing on their own values and previous experiences to enhance their non-verbal signals (body language) and behaviour. This helps them to look and feel more confident and to make the kind of impression on others that they really want to make in any chosen situation.

By adding powerful values-based language, confidence is reinforced by articulating positive thoughts and feelings. Initially, the words used might be internally spoken, through self-talk and affirmations and then externally with others in conversation, presentations etc.

Inputs:

- The coach has an understanding of the coachee's level of confidence and self-esteem from the questions asked in the Issue Identification step of the I-VALUE Coaching Framework

- The coach will also have noted the coachee's body language, attitude, self-perception and verbal language in previous sessions

- The coachee has an understanding of their own level of confidence and self-esteem and has in mind a situation for which they would like to improve their confidence.

Outcomes:

- The coachee learns how to use their values to access inner resources and empower themselves for change, thus living their values every day

- They will learn better body language, thought patterns, behaviours and verbal language to improve how they feel about themselves and how others view them.

Timing:

This technique usually takes around 60 minutes and one or several scenarios can be used.

Tone:

The coach's tone is non-judgemental, engaging and empowering to support the coachee through the changes.

Note:

As the coachee chooses one of their own values for the state they want, it will feel more natural, more like the real them. If they choose a random state, as in traditional NLP, unconnected to their values, this may feel less comfortable and require more 'acting'. It may therefore appear less natural and possibly false, to those around them.

Technique Process:

1. Ask the coachee to choose three values that they are not currently honouring in their lives, particularly in the 'Me to Me' aspect, in a particular situation they are facing.

   Example responses might be: respect, love, acceptance

2. Ask them to access the 'values-based state' they have chosen by thinking of a time when they did honour those values in their lives. If they find that difficult, then ask them to *imagine* a time in the future when they could be honouring those values in their lives.

3. Ask them to keep focused on honouring those values, whilst walking up and down and moving around the room. Notice how they use their physical body, breath, posture, movement and behaviour to show what they are feeling. *Example body language: a smile, softened facial features, head held level, shoulders back and down.*

4. Give the coachee feedback on the changes you noticed to their body language, their posture, movement, behaviour and physical appearance

5. The next step is to add values-based language. Initially introduce this in the language they use with themselves, both self-talk (the way they talk to themselves silently, in their head) and verbal language e.g. affirmations, repeated out loud to themselves.

   Ask the coachee to talk silently to themselves in positive values-based language.

   Then ask them to choose a values-based affirmation that helps them to feel more confident about themselves and repeat it out loud several times. Note down the words chosen. *Example affirmation: I love and accept myself for who I am and I respect my own capabilities.*

6. Finally, ask the coachee to talk to you in values-based language about how they are feeling and how they would approach the situation they had in mind at the beginning of the technique e.g. an interview, date, presentation.

7. Reflect back to the coachee the changes you saw in them, how much more confident they looked and sounded.

8. Ask them to continue to practise the values-based body language and verbal language to embed and sustain their new confident and self-assured state.

Body language examples:

For example, if the coachee chooses a value of 'respect' and they want to create a good impression at a social or networking event, then they can use this technique to access a 'state of respect' by remembering, in detail, a time when they felt really comfortable being respectful to themselves and to others e.g. when talking and listening with friends.

Notice their behaviour, body language and non-verbal signals that showed that respect and then identify changes they can make to create a more respectful impression at this new event. These might include taking care over their appearance, accepting compliments, being punctual, using better eye contact, having a softened facial expression, awareness of others' personal space and showing that they are really listening.

Other examples might be:

- Accessing the value of achievement, act as if they have already achieved the thing they desire by showing passion, excitement, engagement. Appropriate body language might be a big smile, sparkling eyes, assured posture with straight back, shoulders down and chest slightly inflated.
- For a value of support, act in a way that shows support to others. Body language here might include head tilted slightly to one side, nodding appropriately to show they are listening, less body and hand movements.
- With a value of connection, act in a way that makes those connections with others. You might see good eye contact, a smile, use of hand gestures, as appropriate for emphasis, relaxed shoulders and a less formal posture.
- For a value of fun practice having fun in different situations. Good body language would include laughing, smiling, lots of movement and gestures.

Language examples:

Pain-filled words like 'try' and 'hope', allow failure to be an option and lack confidence. Words like 'should' imply an obligation to someone else, not themselves. Using values-based powerful words shows they have confidence in their own ability and certainty that they can get things done, which increases others' confidence in them. Using your values in your language lets others know what is important to you and helps you to focus on the things that really matter to you.

Pain Language:	Value:	Powerful Language:
I'll try and get this done by tomorrow	Achievement	I will enjoy achieving this by tomorrow
I should have time	Reliability	I will make the time to make it happen
It's not my fault	Responsibility	I take responsibility to resolve this
I hope it will be ok	Certainty	I know it will be ok
This is a nightmare	Challenge	This is a challenge I relish

Encourage the coachee to use values-based language in all aspects of their communication, including texts, emails, social media comments, as well as spoken language.

Note: If you use someone's name when talking to them, it strengthens the connection you have made with them and makes them feel valued. Equally, if you get their name wrong, it will make a negative impression and will not make them feel valued.

Affirmation Examples:

When a coachee is choosing an affirmation, they need to make it personal, state it in the present tense and make sure it is positive. Using language based on their values enhances the power of motivation personal to them. Daily repetition of this affirmation will help to make it happen.

Values-Based Affirmation Examples:

Good affirmation examples:

'I have within me, the resources I need to fulfil my purpose'

(Good for someone with a strong value of purpose who has not had the confidence to achieve it)

'I am good at what I do'

139

(Good for someone with a value of capability but who has not been valuing their own capability)

'I love and accept myself for who I am'

(Good for someone with a value of love or acceptance, who wants to improve their self-esteem)

Poor affirmation examples:

'My boss values me'

(Outside your control)

'I will be better at presentations'

(Set in the future, needs to be stated in the present)

'I won't be nervous when networking next week'

(Not stated in the positive)

'He will love me'

(Outside your direct control and not stated in the present)

'I am ok'

(Not values-based so not powerful enough)

Managing Emotions – Increasing Confidence and Self-Esteem

Case Study: Carol - confidence in presenting at a networking group

A business owner in her early thirties was running a successful recruitment agency in the childcare industry and came to me to help her develop her business. She decided to join a networking group but felt really lacking in confidence when she had to stand up and talk about her business.

She read her 60-second presentation to me and looked and sounded very nervous, giving the impression that she was young, inexperienced and unsure of herself. Also, she rushed the words so it was hard to understand.

I asked her to choose three of her core values that were important in this situation and she chose: trust, support and caring.

Focusing on those three values, she brought to mind experiences of working with clients when she was really honouring those values. Just doing that filled her with a 'values glow' and she re-read the 60 seconds, this time looking confident, her eyes showed her supportive and caring nature, rather than the frightened rabbit I had seen earlier. The delivery of her words was more considered, so easier to understand.

Her clothing and appearance made her look a lot younger than she was and so less experienced. She decided to wear more appropriate business attire and wore her long hair up, which made her look older and more professional.

We then worked on the language in the piece and included values-related words, such as caring, supporting, security and protection. She included her level of experience and money-back guarantee to build trust. She added the word 'care' into her company marketing strapline and talked about the support her company offered during the term of the contract.

The next time she presented was much better and each time she did it, she became more and more confident. As a result, people in the group took her seriously and wanted to meet with her to learn more about her business. She began to get more referrals and clients as a result.

Managing Emotions: Reducing Stress

What is stress?

The British Medical Association definition of stress is:

Potentially stressful event(s)	+	Our response to the event(s) (physical, emotional or behavioural)	+	Significance of the event(s) to us (happy, sad, worried or indifferent)	=	Stress

'The significance of the event to us' is the impact it has on our values, positive or negative and the way that makes us feel. The bigger the negative impact is, the bigger the level of stress will be. The greater the number of values affected negatively, the greater the level of stress will be. The higher the priority and level of importance the values that are impacted have for us, the higher the level of stress will be too.

For example: A potentially stressful event might be redundancy. Our response might be shock and we might go around telling everyone about it. The significance of the event and the level of stress we feel depends on the impact this has on our values. So, for example, for someone with core values of *adventure, freedom and choice*, redundancy may have a positive impact on these values. It might give them some funds and the freedom to choose a different career and start a new adventure in their lives. Therefore the level of stress they feel as a result might be quite low.

If however they had core values of *security, fairness, control and responsibility*, then the impact on these values could be very negative and the levels of stress, as a result, could be very high. If they were not expecting the redundancy and it was forced upon them, there would certainly be a big impact on those values of control and fairness. If they were providing for their family and now did not have the means to do so, then the impact on those values of security and responsibility could be quite extreme.

This is the kind of situation that can cause serious anxiety, stress and even depression, if the negative impact continues for a period of time. The emotional and mental stress effects are immediate and over time, physical effects such as stress-related illnesses may develop.

The following technique identifies the emotional stress caused by the significance of the situation to an individual, by understanding the negative impact on their core values.

It supports them in addressing and dealing with the emotion, by drawing on those same values, to respond in a way that reduces the compromise and conflict they feel. This frees them to act in a non-emotional, more rational and practical way, which is helpful for putting an effective plan in place.

By thinking differently about a situation and taking a values-based perspective, they can reduce the negative impact on their values, as the emotion they have attached to the issue lessens.

For example, someone who has a strong value of fairness or justice is in a situation they view as unfair which is causing them to feel stressed. Once they understand which values are affected they can see why they feel the way they do and this frees them to take a different perspective on the situation.

They can look at the possible positive intentions of those involved and what would be fair to them. This may help to reduce the strength of emotion they feel and thus reduce the stress it causes them.

Additionally, they can draw on other values they have, to give them the strength and motivation to take action. It will enhance their confidence and courage to say what needs to be said and do what needs to be done, in the most appropriate and effective way possible to get the best result for all concerned.

The language we use plays a big part in externalising the stress we are feeling. You may notice someone who is feeling stressed, using words like 'nightmare', 'hopeless', 'impossible'. These reinforce their stressed state and show others they are stressed and looking for support. These words can also affect those around them, making them feel more stressed too.

So by encouraging them to use better, more powerful, values-based language, it helps them to express what is important to them. It also helps them to feel calmer, be viewed as a calmer person and will help those around to be calmer too.

Managing Emotions Technique 3: Reducing Stress

Overview:

This technique helps the coachee to reduce their stress levels, by exploring a stressful situation, then identifying the emotional source of their stress. It starts by understanding which of their core values are being dishonoured or receiving a negative impact.

They then use those same values to decide on a course of action that honours their values and so reduces the compromise and conflict they are feeling. Once the emotional response is reduced, their ability to handle things in a rational and effective way is greatly increased.

Often it is the very value that is being compromised in a situation that they need to access and draw on to resolve the situation and reduce the stress they feel. Sometimes drawing on other core values is helpful to strengthen the will to make the necessary changes and take action.

Inputs:

- The coach has the coachee's Values Summary

- The coachee has awareness of a situation that is causing them a great amount of stress.

Outcomes:

- This technique helps people to reduce their stress by understanding their emotional response, through identifying the impact on their core values of a stressful situation

- This then frees them to respond in a way that honours their values, which reduces the stress and supports them in resolving the situation in a more controlled, rational and practical manner.

Timing:

This technique is very flexible and can be completed in 30-60 minutes, depending on how much detail the client needs to include.

Tone:

The coach's tone is supportive, aware that the client may be emotional. The coach also needs to be encouraging and curious to help the coachee through the process.

Note:

Emotion shown by the client is helpful as this means they are working with the right value and that this is a strong value that is important to them.

Technique Process:

1. Ask the coachee to describe the stressful situation they are experiencing and the negative emotions they are feeling e.g. anger, frustration, sadness, anxiety, worry, concern, panic.

2. Ask them to review this in the context of their values and identify which of their core values are being dishonoured or receiving a negative impact.

3. Ask them to reflect on their response in this situation and to identify ways in which they could honour those values in any future response:

   - Help them to identify the choices and options they have to respond to the situation in a non-emotional way.

   - Specifically, ask them to decide who they need to speak to and how they can word the conversation calmly, so they communicate what is important to them and in this way honour their own values.

   - Ask them what they can do differently in their lives and what changes they need to make to enhance the affected values.

4. Ask them to review the actions they decide on to ensure they have a positive impact on all their values. A neutral impact on some is acceptable, however if the planned action has a negative impact on another value, then the action needs to be adjusted. Otherwise further stress could be caused.

5. Ask how they feel about the situation now and when they will start to take action, to gain their commitment to the plan.

Managing Emotions: Reducing Stress

Case Study: Sarah

Sarah, a health professional in her early forties was becoming increasingly stressed as a result of the breakdown in her relationship with the father of her young daughter. The stress she was feeling was affecting her health. She was finding it hard to concentrate on her work and had stopped socialising completely.

In a coaching session, we explored a specific and recent incident to understand the stress she was experiencing and the emotions she was feeling, due to its impact on her values.

We looked at how she was reacting and how she could have behaved differently to achieve a better result.

The incident was triggered by a difference of opinion, with the father of her daughter, over disciplining their daughter on finishing her food. They were all at her ex-partner's house and he had told their daughter she had to finish her food. This was based on his belief that you shouldn't waste good food. Sarah said to her daughter that if she was full she could stop eating. This was based on her belief that over-eating is bad for your health.

Both points of view were valid and the direction to the child was given with good intention. However, because of their heightened emotional state, due to the breakdown of their relationship, this caused an angry and painful argument between the parents, who both felt they were in the right.

In taking a values approach to the situation, first we looked at which of her own values Mum, Sarah, was dishonouring in giving their child a different instruction to the one her Dad had, only moments before. She quickly realised she was being inconsiderate and unfair to both Dad and their daughter, by over-ruling him and giving an inconsistent message to their daughter. So the identified values were *consideration* and *fairness*.

147

Her response at the time, when he told her she shouldn't have said that, was to accuse him of not supporting her in raising their daughter well. Her core value here was *support*. However once she could see how her response dishonoured her own, as well as his values, then she could easily see how she could have responded differently to get a better result.

To resolve the situation, she agreed to arrange to meet Dad, when their daughter was not present, to discuss it. Drawing on her own values, she felt able to apologise for the lack of consideration and fairness she had shown during this incident. She was able to acknowledge his positive intention to help their daughter to value the things she has and his differing beliefs over the importance of finishing a meal and not wasting good food.

This acknowledgement helped him to listen to her as she expressed her opinion as a health professional. Her view was that it is important to stop eating when you are full to avoid over-eating which puts a strain on the digestive system.

They were then able to agree a new and consistent approach in their parenting methods which honoured her value of support for each other and their daughter.

By showing respect and consideration, while acknowledging his point of view, she was honouring their respective values. This made it easier for him to respond in a helpful way so they could both act with integrity and create a supportive environment for their child. This reduced the stress for everyone.

Vitality

Making Change with Values

The third section of the 'L' step: 'Living a Values-Led Life' in the I-VALUE Coaching Framework is about learning how to use values to make change. This includes:

- Decision-making and prioritising
- Problem-solving
- Action planning

These techniques bring values into every day activities, by using them for making better decisions, prioritising the right things, solving problems and planning action to put in place the change needed to live a values-led life.

When coaching someone to make decisions and plan actions, it is essential to review the impact of the decision or action on all their core values. This is important to ensure the impact is positive and not negative in any way. It can leave the values neutral.

Honouring a value means having a positive impact on it. Dishonouring a value means having a negative impact on it. Leaving it neutral means having no impact on the value.

If the impact is negative, then taking that decision and that action will not lead to a strong sense of happiness or fulfilment. Something will be missing or there will be a sense of doubt or worry, which may lead them to reverse the decision at a later stage or give up on it altogether. So some adjustment will be needed to remove any negative impact on their values.

When people make values-based decisions, they have certainty that the decisions will be right for them, as they are honouring their values. This helps to stop procrastination and fear of failure because they learn to trust their own judgement. The same is true of prioritising. Using values to guide prioritisation means they will always get it right and so there is more certainty and less fear and worry about what to do first.

Planning action and making change that is in line with their values means they are constantly making progress towards the goal of living a values-led life. So again there is certainty, a sense of purpose and trust in the knowledge that they are on the right path.

Making Change Technique 1: Decision-Making and Prioritising

Overview:

This technique helps the coachee to make better values-based decisions and helps them to prioritise things in the best way for them.

It can be used for minor and major decisions on trivial or life-changing matters.

It is good practice for everyone to use their values for decision-making and prioritising to ensure they are living their life in line with their values. It is particularly helpful for people who procrastinate, worry or stress about decisions or who have made bad decisions in the past and are fearful of making more.

Inputs:

- The coach has the coachee's Values Summary

- The coachee has awareness of a decision or a prioritisation that they have to make, that they may have been worrying about or putting off.

Outcomes:

- This technique helps people to make good decisions and prioritise more effectively, thus helping them to progress more quickly towards achieving their goals and attaining the things they aim for in life

- This realises their potential and enhances their sense of happiness and feelings of fulfilment that come with living a values-led life.

Timing:

This technique is very flexible and can be completed in 10-30 minutes, depending on how much detail the client needs to include.

Tone:

The coach's tone can be supportive or challenging depending on which is most helpful to the coachee.

Note:

The impact on all the coachee's core values needs to be reviewed at the end of the technique to ensure none of their values are being dishonoured in any way. If this is the case, then the option chosen needs to be adjusted so the impact is at least neutral.

The example given is for decision-making however the same process applies for prioritising. For the latter, allow more focus on the level of importance of the values affected i.e. their prioritisation within the Top 10 core values. For example, honour the 1-3 numbered values above the 7-10 values.

Technique Process:

1. Identify the decision or prioritisation to be made. This may have been identified in the first coaching session in the Issue Identification step of the I-VALUE Coaching Framework and it is now time to address it.

   Example: Ali, an IT professional in his forties, seeking career coaching has to make a decision about whether to stay doing contract work or apply for a permanent position. He has been putting off the decision for a while. His contract has now ended, so he has to decide which kinds of roles to apply for.

2. Review, with the coachee, their core values and ask them whether each option honours, dishonours or leaves neutral each value.

   Example response: Contracting honours my values of worldliness, knowledge and adventure, as I gain experience in many different companies and environments. It dishonours security, loyalty, recognition and trust as I am not at one company for long and am always having to focus on getting the next job. It leaves the rest of my values neutral. A permanent role would honour security, loyalty, trust, worldliness, knowledge, recognition. It would leave two others neutral but I think there will be less adventure and a possible impact on wellbeing, as I might not be able to go to the gym so often.

3. Ask the coachee to decide which is the best option for them, based on living their life in line with their values.
   Example response: Going for a permanent role is definitely the right option. It enhances loads more values. Security is my number one value and I have very little of that at the moment. It's a constant worry for me.

4. Now ask the coachee what adjustments they can make to remove any possible negative impact of the remaining values.

   Example response: There will be less adventure from the role itself, as I'll just be at one company, but I will actually be able to take proper holidays. So I guess I can honour that value in a different way by choosing an adventurous holiday. My wife and I have always talked about going on a safari, now's my chance! I was worried about not being able to go to the gym, but if I'm working proper hours, I can go in the evening and actually taking holidays will enhance my wellbeing. While I'm contracting I don't take holidays as I don't get paid and when my contract ends I'm worried about the money running out, so won't spend any. That has to change.

5. Ask how they feel about the decision now and when they will start to take action.

   Example response: Decision made! I'm going for it, I'll start looking for permanent roles as soon as I get home. That's such a relief!

Making Change: Decision-Making and Prioritising

Case study: Amelia

A woman in her late thirties was working with me on growing her business, when one of the barriers to success she identified was that she didn't know where she would be living. She and her partner had mentioned buying a place but nothing had been decided and nothing was moving forward. In the meantime, she felt she couldn't make any decisions about her business.

We looked at which was the biggest priority for her, growing her business or moving house and the impact of these two choices on her Top 10 Core Values.

Growing her business honoured her number 1 value of Making a Difference and also her values of Wellbeing, Recognition and Learning. She had previously felt that she wanted them to buy a flat together to give her a stronger sense of Stability (value 9) and also Commitment (value 8) from him to the relationship.

However, moving to another area, as they couldn't afford to buy near where they were renting, would have a negative impact on her values of Sense of Belonging and Stability. She would lose her local support network of friends and colleagues and she would probably lose a lot of clients too. So there would be a negative impact on her top value of Making a Difference and also Wellbeing as a result.

Just by reviewing these priorities in light of her core values she was able to identify exactly what her priorities were. She wanted to grow the business in that area, so to do this she would draw on her value of Honesty and have an open discussion with her partner. She would explain how important it was for her to be able to develop her business where they were.

When she next approached the subject of moving house, she could manage her emotions and have a rational and practical discussion with her partner, being honest about what she wanted and listening to his thoughts.

They now have agreed a way forward and have a plan of action which she is happy with and which honours her values of Stability and Sense of Belonging. She feels they can talk more openly and she feels more Commitment in the relationship.

Her confidence has grown in terms of making the right decisions and prioritising the right things. She is now free to develop her business and has moved past the barriers in her mind that were holding her back.

Making Change: Problem-Solving

In every day life, whether at home or at work, we face problems,
challenges and issues. Using a values-based approach to solving them
plays a big part in learning to live a values-led life.

This technique takes a different perspective on problem solving and
helps to look at a situation in a new light and so tackle it in a different way.

It uses the concepts of 'framing' and 'reframing', which are used in
Neuro Linguistic Programming (NLP). Framing is the way we describe
our experiences to give them meaning. So reframing is the process
of changing the frame we put on something to give it a different
meaning. This new meaning helps to make the issue more acceptable
and manageable and so a solution is easier to find.

This technique helps the coachee to view a situation or issue with a
'values-based outcome frame' rather than a 'problem frame'. This
enables them to see things from a different perspective and understand
other people's perceptions. In doing so, it allows the coachee to
remove the emotion from a situation and handle it more rationally and
effectively, thus reducing the conflict and stress it has caused.

A 'problem frame':

-   focuses on the problems to be avoided
-   motivates away from negative consequences
-   describes what is not wanted, what to stay away from, what
    to remove.

A 'values-based outcome frame':

-   focuses on values-based goals to be achieved
-   motivates through values
-   describes what is wanted and desired.

It can be used for any kind of problem, minor or major, in any aspect
of life.

The coach may wish to refer back to the 'Issue Identification' step or the Awareness Summary completed at the end of the 'A' step: Awareness of Self and Change Needed of the I-VALUE Coaching Framework. At those points specific problems or issues raised by the coachee would have been noted and could now be addressed using this technique.

Alternatively, there may be specific problems that the coachee brings to a coaching session that they want to focus on.

Making Change Technique 2: Problem-Solving

Overview:

This technique gives a new perspective on problems and helps to turn problems into values-based outcomes. This approach turns conflict into opportunity and helps to resolve problems more effectively and efficiently. It works by reframing a problem and putting it into a values-based outcome frame.

Inputs:

- The coach has the coachee's Values Summary and the outcome frame questions

- The coach may also have issues raised from the coachee's earlier sessions e.g. those captured on the Awareness Summary

- The coachee has awareness of a problem, challenge or issue that is causing conflict or stress which needs to be resolved.

Outcomes:

- Improved understanding of the situation by taking a values perspective

- Enhanced communication leading to faster progress and better solutions

- Increased motivation, engagement and ownership of the issue

- Improved use of time, energy, resources and effort.

Timing:

This technique is very flexible and can be completed in 20-30 minutes and can take place in any coaching session, after the Awareness step of the I-VALUE Coaching Framework.

Tone:

The coach's tone is challenging, questioning and curious to help the coachee to take a different perspective.

Note:

This technique can be used to produce a positive Goal statement which can be taken forward in the GROW with Values technique to produce options and a way forward for the coachee. (See Goal-Setting Technique 2: GROW with Values earlier in the 'L' step: Living a Values-Led Life of the Framework).

Technique Process:

- Coach asks the coachee what the problem, issue or challenge is that they want to focus on. The coachee may need prompting from the list of issues captured in earlier sessions. This gives the problem frame.

- Coach asks the coachee to reframe the problem with a values-based outcome frame, by asking the following numbered questions:

Example issue: David, a property management company owner in his fifties had found that he gets angry and frustrated very easily about things in the work environment. Recently, he had a new tenant coming into one of his properties and things had been taking a while to progress. He had received an email from the estate agent saying that David was completely at fault for everything taking so long. He felt this was grossly unfair and not at all justified.

1. Which of your core values are important in this situation?

   Example response: The core value that is important in this situation is fairness and an action like this is a direct hit on that value.

2. Which value do you want to enhance?

   Example response: Fairness

3. How will you know when you have achieved that?

   (Be specific, what will you see, hear feel?)

   Example response: I would have achieved honouring that value if I could hear myself talking calmly to the person involved and not shouting and screaming at them. It would feel better and I would get a better result.

4. Which other core values can you draw on to help you achieve this outcome?

   Example response: I also want to draw on my value of respect, I think this would help.

5. What have you succeeded with before that is similar?
   Example response: I honour these values with my family when I speak to them, but I recognise that I am not honouring them at work.

6. What is the next step?

   Example response: My next step is to keep calm, be fair to the other person and hear their point of view before responding.

David's values-based outcome frame is:

'*To be fair in my treatment of others at work*'.

Making Change: Action Planning

Action planning is the final section of the 'L' step: Living a Values-Led Life in the I-VALUE Coaching Framework.

Two techniques are described to explore the change needed and identify a plan of action to make it happen. Both are aligned to values to ensure that the action planned is moving the coachee forward towards living their life in line with their core values. This supports increasing future happiness and fulfilment once the action plan is complete and the changes made.

The first technique is a simple change model, which starts with the values-based goal, then looks at the current position to identify the change needed.

The second technique is the 'start, stop, continue' process which identifies specific values-based actions, activities or behaviours that the coachee wants to start doing, stop doing or continue doing.

These techniques can be used effectively as stand-alone techniques or they can be used one after the other, in the order in which they are presented here.

From a coaching perspective, a key part of the process is the follow-up step. It is essential that the coach follows-up with the coachee to review their progress with the changes and actions agreed from these techniques.

They are simple techniques, but the power comes in the implementation. The coach needs to hold the coachee accountable for completing them either by follow-up email/phone call or in the following coaching session. This ensures the benefit is received and progress is made by the coachee.

Making Change Technique 3: Action Planning: 3-Step Change Model

Overview:

This technique can be used to focus on one issue, value or aspect of life or work to identify changes needed. It uses a simple 3-step change process. It is useful to help a coachee to develop a plan of action when time does not allow to go through a full GROW with Values model. It is possible to make good progress with a simpler model.

Inputs:

- The coach has the coachee's Wheel of Life, values, issues and areas for change noted down in the Awareness Summary Template from the first and second coaching sessions

- The coachee has an awareness of the areas for change and a commitment to make change.

Outcomes:

- The coach provides a summary for the coachee of their agreed values-based actions

- The coachee gives a commitment to take action to begin the changes they want to make to live a values-led life.

Timing:

This technique usually takes around 20-30 minutes and could be completed in any coaching session once the 'A' step: Awareness of Self and Change Needed of the I-VALUE Coaching Framework is completed.

Tone:

The coach's tone is encouraging and supportive and challenging, where appropriate, while the coachee identifies the changes they need to make.

Note:

This technique could be used with any number of issues, values or areas for change. However care should be taken not to overload the coachee with actions in one session.

It can also be followed immediately by the next technique to identify more specific actions to take forward.

Actions need to be reviewed against all the coachee's core values at the end of the exercise to ensure none of their values are being dishonoured in any way. If this is the case, then actions need to be adjusted so the impact is at least neutral.

3 Step Change Model

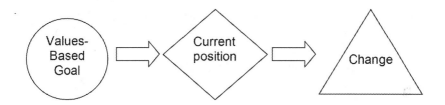

(Adapted from Valle and Bandler's NLP Process for Change 1994)

Technique Process:

Coach: presents the key aspects of life or work, values or issues identified from the 'I', 'V' and 'A' steps of the Framework, that have been noted as areas to focus on in the Awareness Summary.

Coachee: chooses one aspect, value or issue on which to start making changes.

Coach: asks the coachee to identify their value-based goal in respect of this aspect/issue in their life.

Example question:

-   *With your values in mind, what do you want to achieve?*

Coach: asks the coachee to summarise their current position in respect of this aspect/issue.

Example question:

-   *How is that different from what you are doing now? or Where are you now?*

Coach: asks the coachee what change they need to make.

Example question:

-   *What could you change? or What could you do differently?*

Note: The coach must allow the coachee to come up with their own ideas and plan of action, rather than suggesting solutions or direction themselves.

The coach notes down the actions identified from the answers to the questions. The coach then asks the coachee to review the actions agreed to ensure that they all honour the coachee's core values.

They may leave some values neutral i.e. have no impact on them and this is acceptable. However, if any actions have a negative impact on any values then the actions will need to be adjusted to neutralise the impact. If this is not done, it will be counter-productive, as new issues will arise when a core value is being dishonoured.

The coach then produces a summary for the coachee to use themselves to start making the changes, by taking the actions in the timescales agreed.

The coach then follows up on those actions at the next coaching session, to see what progress has been made.

Making Change Technique 4: Action Planning: Start, Stop, Continue

Overview:

This technique can be used to focus on one issue, value or aspect of life/work to identify changes needed. It uses a simple 'start, stop, continue' process.

Inputs:

- The coach has the coachee's Wheel of Life, values, issues and areas for change noted down in the Awareness Summary from the first and second coaching sessions

- The coachee has an awareness of the areas for change and a commitment to make change.

Outcomes:

- The coach provides a summary for the coachee of their agreed actions to start, stop and continue

- The coachee gives a commitment to take action to begin the changes they want to make in their lives.

Timing:

This technique usually takes around 20-30 minutes and could be completed in any coaching session after the 'Awareness' step of the Framework is completed.

Tone:

The coach's tone is encouraging and supportive and challenging where appropriate as the coachee identifies the changes they need to make.

Note:

This technique could be used with any number of issues, values or areas for change. However care should be taken not to overload the coachee with actions in one session.

Actions agreed need to be reviewed against all the coachee's core values at the end of the exercise to ensure that none of their values is being dishonoured in any way. If this is the case, then actions need to be adjusted to remove the negative impact.

Technique Process:

The coach presents to the coachee, the key aspects of life or work, values or issues identified from the 'I', 'V' and 'A' steps of the Framework, that have been noted as areas to focus on in the Awareness Summary.

The coachee then chooses one aspect, value or issue to start making changes.

Start: Coach asks:

'What do you need to start doing or saying to honour this value and effect change in this aspect of your life or issue, as appropriate?

'With your values in mind... who do you need to start being?'

'... who do you need to start having in your life?'

'... where do you need to start going or being for this to happen?'

'... when do you need to start doing these things?'

'... how does this start happening?'

Stop: Coach asks:

'What do you need to stop doing or saying that is dishonouring this value and causing this issue in your life?'

'Who do you need to stop being?'

'Who else do you need to stop being present in your life?'

'Where do you need to stop going or being for this to happen?'

'When do you need to stop doing these things?'

'How does this stop happening?'

Continue: Coach asks:

'What do you need to continue doing or saying that is already honouring this value and will help to make change in this aspect of your life?'

'Who do you need to continue being?'

'Who do you need to continue to have in your life?'

'Where do you need to continue going or being to support this change?'

'When do you need to continue doing these things?'

'How does this continue happening?'

The coach must allow the coachee to come up with their own ideas and plan of action, rather than suggesting solutions or direction themselves.

The coach notes down the actions identified from the answers to the questions. The coach then asks the coachee to review the actions agreed to ensure that they all honour the coachee's core values.

Some values may receive no impact. However, if the actions planned have a negative impact on any core values then the actions will need to be adjusted. Otherwise it will be counter-productive, as new issues will arise if a core value is being dishonoured.

The coach then produces a summary for the coachee to use to start making the changes, by taking the actions in the timescales agreed. The coach then follows up on those actions at the next coaching session, to see what progress has been made.

U   Understanding the Values of Others

Once a good understanding of values has been established and the coachee is taking action to live a values-led life, they can then progress to understand the values of others in their lives.

We can enhance our communication and deepen our relationships by being able to identify other people's values and honour their values in the way we behave towards them.

If we do not understand the values of those around us, our communication tends to happen at a behavioural level, e.g. he said, she said, without awareness of people's true motivation and reasoning. Our relationships may be operating at a more superficial level, based on assumptions and judgements, without an understanding of what really matters to each other.

The 'U' step in the I-VALUE Coaching Framework is for Understanding the Values of Others.

For the coachee, this can be about understanding the values of anyone in their lives, whether at home, at work, socially and in their community. This may be their partner, their parents, their children, family members and friends. It might also be work colleagues, their boss and their clients, anyone with whom they communicate.

This step in the Framework includes understanding how other people's communication affects the coachee and whether it has a positive or negative impact on their values and the feelings generated.

It also includes understanding how to use values in language and communication with others. This can be extremely empowering and also attractive to others. Using values-based language can make a big difference to the effectiveness of communication in relationships.

Specific coaching sessions could be used to enhance a presentation or some marketing material to tap into the values of the audience, build rapport, motivate others and attract success.

At the end of this step in the framework, the coachee will have a good understanding of how to elicit the values of other people in their lives. Additionally, they will know how to use values in their communication to build stronger and more lasting relationships.

This step is usually completed in one or two coaching sessions, after the 'L' step of the Framework.

Do you use values-based language in your relationships?

Understand the values of another and you know them well; communicate in values-based language and you know each other well.

Understanding the Values of Others Technique 1: Identification of the Values of Others

Overview:

This technique is particularly useful for understanding the values of others around you; clients, your partner, family members, friends, peers, team members etc. without a formal values discussion.

Our core values are individual to us. We all have different backgrounds upbringings and experiences, in the diverse environment in which we live and work. It is important therefore to understand the values of others, to understand what is important to them and engage with them more effectively.

Values provide us with the unconscious reason 'why' we behave and react as we do. It is useful to understand what will bring happiness and fulfilment to others when their values are honoured and sadness, frustration or anger, when missing or dishonoured.

Inputs:

- The coach brings a knowledge of values and the set of questions to the session

- The coachee has someone in mind that they would like to understand better.

Outcomes:

- Identification of the core values of the person the coachee has chosen to focus on. These values can then be used in other techniques to build rapport, improve communication and enhance the relationship.

Timing:

This exploration technique is flexible and takes around 30 minutes and would be completed in the fourth or later coaching session in a programme.

Tone:

The coach's tone is enquiring, encouraging and authoritative. The coachee will expect the coach to be knowledgeable on whether a word is a value or not. They may also look to the coach to help them find the right word. So, offering some encouraging input and options may be helpful.

Note:

Depending on how well the coachee knows the person they have chosen, they may need to understand the technique in the session, then take it away and use it when they next see that person.

Technique Process:

Observe:

The first step is for the coachee to observe the person whose values they want to understand. If they know them well, then ask them to recall examples of behaviour they have observed from this person. If they don't, then they may need to take this away as an action and discuss it in the next session.

Ask them to describe a time when they have seen this person very happy and another time when they have seen them very angry, frustrated or sad.

For each situation, ask them what they think is important to the person that caused them to respond in that way. If they were observing a negative emotion, ask them what is important to the person that was missing in the situation.

Help them to identify potential core values of the person and note them down.

Listen:

The next step is for the coachee to listen to the language the person uses. Again, if they know the person well, ask them to recall their conversations, particularly ones that were emotionally charged. It is helpful if they can remember the exact words used and not their own interpretation.

If they can't recall specific conversations, then they may need to take this away as an action and discuss it in the next session.

Ask the coachee to recall the words used and help them to identify the person's potential core values that get mentioned and note them down.

Questions to ask in conversation:

If the coachee is comfortable with actually asking the person about their values, then they can ask the following questions. They may need to ask the question several times to get to the heart of what is important.

- *'What do you value in life/work?*

- *'What is most important to you?'*

- *'What does that give you?'*

- *'What else?'*

Or in a negative situation, ask: *'What is important to you that was missing in that situation, or that person's behaviour?'*

Note: The coachee needs to help the person to identify one word that sums up each value for them and they need to note it down, using the person's words, not their own and bring them to the next session. The coachee will really need to understand values to be able to do this, so experience of working with their own values is needed before they will be able to understand those of others.

Through observing, listening and questioning, it is possible for the coachee to identify a person's core values and thus understand them so much better.

Values examples in language:

If someone is recounting a negative incident, watch out for the value that was missing for them. You might hear them saying, 'some people have no respect'; or 'it's just not fair'; or 'nobody could care less about me' – so values that are important to them are evident: **respect; fairness; caring.**

If they are talking about a positive scenario, it will be the value that matters to them that you will hear. For example, you might hear someone say, 'I feel safe when I'm with him'; 'she really appreciated what I did for her'; 'I know I can really trust him' – clear values here are **safety; appreciation; trust.**

Example scenario:

If the coachee manages someone who hates the job they do, their focus, as a manager, may be on setting goals/agreeing actions to help them find another job. However, they could be moving to a very similar environment that they might also not enjoy, unless they first establish why they don't enjoy their job.

Using a values-based approach means exploring why they feel the way they do. Finding which values in their work environment are not being honoured, then taking action to honour them. Thus improving the situation and their motivation.

Through listening and questioning, the coachee might have observed that their member of staff has a strong value of recognition, which is not currently being honoured at work. So by focusing on enhancing this value with them, options may present themselves e.g.

- finding opportunities to give praise to others in the team may encourage others to give praise back;
- having regular appraisal meetings with them to give appropriate recognition;
- setting up a recognition trophy in the team and awarding it to the most supportive colleague each week;
- scheduling a time in team meetings where everyone has the opportunity to recognise something good about someone else on the team.

Lindsay West

Even just one of these changes could make a big difference to that individual's working environment and whether their value of recognition is honoured. This would enhance their motivation to work hard and stay at the company. It would no doubt improve the office for others too and make it a better place to work for the whole team.

Understanding the Values of Others Technique 2: Using the Values of Others to Enhance Communication, Rapport, Motivation and Relationships

Once the coachee has identified a person's values, using the previous technique, then they can adjust their own language and behaviour to honour that person's values. This is helpful for communicating at a deeper level, establishing rapport, motivating others and building good relationships, whether personal or business.

Rapport occurs when two people feel they are 'in sync' or 'on the same wavelength'. They have made a connection because they feel similar or can relate to each other. There are a number of techniques used to establish rapport e.g. body language, eye contact etc. Here we will be using the language of values to make that crucial connection.

People's values are their motivators and the drivers that influence their decisions, choices and reactions. It is important to respect and honour the values of others. By actively doing this, it is possible to enhance their motivation and even their self-esteem. Results are achieved by honouring, rather than challenging, someone's values.

Understanding the Values of Others Technique 2: Using the Values of Others to Enhance Communication, Rapport, Motivation and Relationships

Overview:

In this technique we look at how changing the language we use can make a big difference to honouring the values of others and thus enhancing the relationship through deeper communication.

Values-based communication establishes rapport quickly, taps into motivational drivers, removes conflict and generally strengthens relationships through making a deeper connection. Giving positive values-based feedback is so much more powerful than behaviour-based feedback, in terms of motivation.

Inputs:

- The coach brings a knowledge of values, language, behaviour, rapport, motivation and relationships

- The coachee has an understanding of the values of a person with whom they want to improve their relationship.

Outcomes:

- The coach enhances the coachee's knowledge of how to use values to build rapport, motivate and enhance relationships

- The coachee learns the knowledge and skills to improve their communication using values to build rapport, motivate, remove conflict and improve their relationships.

Timing:

This technique is flexible and takes around 30 minutes and would be completed in the fourth or later coaching session in a programme, once the coachee is really familiar with values. It is used directly after the previous technique to understand someone else's values.

Tone:

The coach's tone is supportive and authoritative. The coachee may look to the coach to assist them in finding the right words. So, offering some encouraging input and options may be helpful.

Note:

When adjusting their language and behaviour to honour someone else's values, the coachee must ensure they continue to honour their own values too. If they acted against their own values, they would be uncomfortable and unhappy. Their behaviour would appear incongruent, inconsistent and not authentic, so this would not enhance the relationship.

It is important to use the motivation technique **only with positive feedback**. Negative feedback should be given based on behaviour and NOT on values. A challenge on someone's values is not helpful and will definitely not motivate them.

Technique Process:

This technique uses 'role play' where the coach plays the part of the person with whom the coachee wants to build rapport, improve communication, enhance motivation and strengthen the relationship. The coachee plays themselves.

The coachee learns how to adjust their language to honour the other person's values. They can then use values-based language with the person in reality, after the session.

The coachee has already established some of the core values of the other person using the previous technique and will now practice using those values in their language in conversation with them.

Example

The coachee has identified the values of the person, they want to focus on, as:

- Appreciation

- Honesty

- Fairness

- Commitment

- Respect

Communication and Rapport

The coach initiates the 'role play' conversation re-enacting a work scenario, by saying:

'I just can't believe the way I'm being treated, it's not fair!'

Ask the coachee to respond using the person's values in their language e.g.:

*'Being treated **fairly** is important, what happened?'*

The coach responds:

'They didn't tell me they needed the report today, I always deliver on time and now it makes me look bad because it's not ready!'

Ask the coachee to respond again using the person's values in their language e.g. *'That sounds very **unfair**, they weren't being **honest** with you about the urgency. I really **appreciate** how **committed** you are to achieving your deadlines. I am sure people will understand and **respect** that you weren't told. How much more time do you need?'*

Coach responds based on how they now feel:

'Well actually I only need another couple of hours. Thanks for understanding I'm much calmer now. I'll go and explain.'

In this example, by using the person's values in their language, the coachee made the person feel understood. They made a connection that was deeper and more meaningful, thus establishing rapport and building their relationship.

This person may well turn to the coachee again and so the bond of understanding is created.

Motivation

To motivate this person, the coachee can give them values-based feedback specifically mentioning one of the values that are important to the individual. This enhances that value and will immediately make them feel good. Using the language of their values is like pulling the trigger on their motivation.

Taking their core value of **appreciation**, the coachee can practise giving them values-based feedback starting with... *'I really **appreciate** you for...'* which is much more powerful than behaviour-based feedback such as: *'you did a great job'*.

Showing values-based appreciation, even for small things, will really motivate them. Equally, they will become very demotivated if they do not feel appreciated and are taken for granted. So by creating an environment of appreciation, by saying '*thank you*' often and '*I appreciate…*', they will thrive.

If the person raised an issue, the coachee could respond '*I value your **honesty** in raising this and I **appreciate** your **commitment** to finding a solution…*'rather than '*Ok, what do you plan to do about this issue?*'

If there was a conflict situation, to motivate them to resolve it, the coachee could say, '*to be **fair** to all parties and **respect**ing each other's point of view, let's see how we can resolve this position…*' rather than '*we need to find a compromise*'.

To motivate the person to achieve a deadline, the coachee could say, '*I know with your **commitment**, you will make this happen*', rather than '*I know you'll get it done.*'

Relationships

The same technique can be applied in personal relationships too. If the person the coachee has chosen has a core value of respect, they can adjust their language to honour that value.

For example, they can give positive feedback by saying, '*I really respect the way you handled that*', or '*I completely respect your decision to…*' rather than just saying, '*well done*' or '*I agree*'.

If their partner complains about their share of the chores, saying, '*it's not fair*', rather than saying '*ok, what do you want me to do?*' They could give a values-based response and say '*I would like you to feel the chores are shared fairly. What changes do we need to make?*'

Enhancing Communication: presentations and marketing

A values-based communications approach can be applied in any context.

For a successful presentation the coachee needs to think about the values of their audience and tap into them in the language used in the presentation. This will get their attention, make a connection and attract them to the concept.

From a marketing perspective, they would need to think about the values of their target market and use those words in any marketing communication, whether it is a website, a leaflet, a business card or a TV advertisement. Using values-based language that is relevant to your audience is extremely powerful in attracting new clients and building a business.

Summary

In summary, understanding the values of those around us is very important in understanding them better. Using language based on their values is a very powerful communication technique for establishing rapport, enhancing motivation and building successful relationships, in any context.

Friendship

E   Evaluating Progress

To complete the coaching programme, a period of reflection and evaluation is needed. This allows the coachee to see how much they have achieved and how far they have come from their first session.

Without this, the coachee may think they have made some progress. However, often they will have forgotten how bad things were when they started the coaching. They may therefore not appreciate just *how* much progress they have made.

The final step of the I-VALUE Coaching Framework is therefore 'E' for Evaluating Progress.

This takes place as a review of the Wheel of Life scores and the Values scores. (See the following completed examples.) An evaluation of progress is undertaken against expectations and planned accomplishments stated in the first session of the programme and against Ideal Life plans and agreed actions from various techniques used during the coaching programme.

At the end of this step in the process, the coach and coachee will have clearly identified the level of progress made. This is based on the coachee's feelings about how closely they are living their life aligned to their values and their satisfaction with each aspect of their lives.

It will also be based on the successful resolution of identified issues and problems they have worked on during the course of the programme.

Any new or outstanding areas for development identified from this review can be taken back to the start of the I-VALUE Coaching Framework once again to identify the issues. So the process of coaching and development continues: as one cycle of the framework ends, the next one begins.

This final step of the I-VALUE Coaching Framework is completed at the end of the last coaching session in the programme.

Are you measuring the right things?

**Measure completion of goals, you'll find completed goals;
measure enhancement of values, you'll find happiness.**

Evaluated Wheel of Life Example

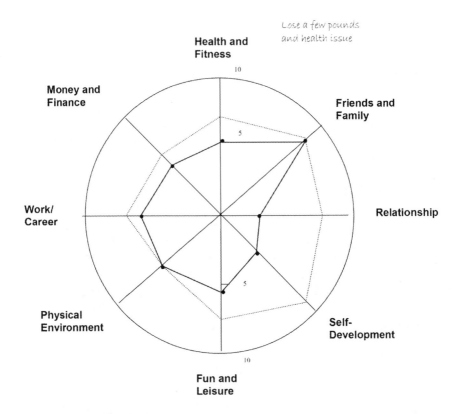

Mark each line on the scale of 1-10, in terms of your satisfaction with that area of your life (1 is low, 10 is high), then join each mark to the next to show the wheel of your life. Then reflect on how smooth a ride you are having right now and in which areas of your life you would like to make changes to increase your satisfaction levels.

Area for Change:	Current Score: Date: xx/xx/xx	Target Score:	Achieved Score: Date: xx/xx/xx
Health and Fitness	5	8	7
Relationship	3	8	8
Self Development	4	8	9

Evaluated Values Summary Example

Priority Number	Core Value	Interpretation	Score and Target Score	Achieved Score
1-10	*What's important to you? Enter core values here:*	*What does that mean to you? What does that give you?*	*How are you living your life in line with your values? Score 0-10 → Target Score*	
1	Happiness	Enjoyment, pleasure, excitement, variety, sense of humour	6 → 10	8
=1	Being Valued	Acceptance, inner strength, courage, commitment	5 → 8	9
3	Wellbeing	Energy, feeling good, relaxation, development, improvement	6 → 9	8
=3	Trust	Loyalty	5 → 10	7
=3	Honesty	Openness, loyalty	5 → 9	7
6	Friendship	Understanding, connection, support, kindness, sharing, familiarity	7 → 9	9
7	Love	Closeness, connection, support, kindness, caring	6 → 10	9

8	Stability	Security, balance, consistency, sense of control, commitment, discipline, routine	5 → 10	**8**
9	Recognition	Appreciation, external validation, achievement	5 → 7	**9**
10	Respect	Fairness, consideration, moderation, professionalism	6 → 8	**8**

Summary of Part 2

I Issue Identification

Seek first to understand, then you will be understood.

V Values Exploration

'Values are like fingerprints, nobody's are the same but you leave 'em all over everything you do.' Elvis Presley

A Awareness of Self and Change Needed

'Your vision will become clear only when you can look into your own heart. Who looks outside, dreams; who looks inside, awakens.' C.G. Jung

L Living a Values-Led Life

Understanding your values gives clarity, living your values brings happiness.

U Understanding the Values of Others

Understand the values of another and you know them well; communicate in values-based language and you know each other well.

E Evaluating Progress

Measure completion of goals, you'll find completed goals; measure enhancement of values, you'll find happiness.

Conclusion

I really appreciate that you have taken the time to read 'Coaching with Values' to completion and I trust that you have enjoyed it.

It would give me great pleasure if you were to use the framework and techniques presented, in your coaching practice with your clients and colleagues. Please do share your successes, ideas and questions with me and other coaches in the Facebook Group: **Values Coaching Community.**

If you are interested in attending the Values Coach Training Programme and/or would like to be considered for joining my team of Values Coaches, please do get in touch at **lindsay@valuescoach. co.uk**. We are building an international team, delivering Values Coaching worldwide.

For more information on workshops and training courses in which to practise the techniques from this book in a safe and supportive environment, please go to our website:

www.valuescoach.co.uk

How much of a difference do you make to the lives of the people you coach?

Could you make a bigger difference by coaching with values?

Coaching makes a difference;
Coaching with values makes a bigger difference.

Achievement

Values Resources

Values Coach UK www.valuescoach.co.uk

Values Coach UK provide and range of values-based coaching and training programmes, webinars, workshops, resources and events. These are delivered by Lindsay West and her team of values coaches, who have all completed the Values Coach Training Programme.

Lindsay and her team are committed to providing high quality services and supporting clients in achieving excellent results. Values are at the heart of everything they do. They are passionate about helping individuals and organisations to understand and live their values everyday.

Here are details of other organisations with a focus on values:

The UK Values Alliance www.valuesalliance.net

The UK Values Alliance is a collaborative group that is seeking to promote values in society. They formed as a result of the UK National Values Survey, which demonstrated a large gap between the personal values of UK residents and the values they see at a national level.

They are a hub for individuals and organisations active or interested in the field of values. Their belief is that by acting together, they can make a bigger difference than they can by acting alone.

Their stated purpose is to build a better UK society by helping individuals and organisations be more aware of, understand and live their values.

Lindsay West is on the Steering Group of the UK Values Alliance

Barrett Values Centre www.valuescentre.com

At the Barrett Values Centre they are committed to furthering and deepening the collective understanding of the evolution of human consciousness.

They are committed to remain specialized in the field of values, whole system change, and personal and cultural transformation.

They provide powerful metrics that enable leaders to measure and manage the cultures of their organizations, and the leadership development needs of their managers and leaders.

The core products of the organisation are the Cultural Transformation Tools.

Human Values Foundation www.humanvaluesfoundation.com

The Human Values Foundation offers programmes to schools and youth-related organisations enabling children and young people to understand the crucial importance of positive values and learn how to practise them in every aspect of their lives, so developing the personal, emotional and social skills that will help them live a fulfilled and constructive life.

my31practices web app www.my31practices.com

Release the power of your personal values every day with this great web app. You can use my31Practices to translate your values into very practical actions and behaviours. You focus on just one practice each day.

References

Page Number:	Reference:
Page 6	1. Rokeach, Milton (1973) *The Nature of Human Values*. New York: The Free Press
Page 20	2. Covey, S.R. (2004) *The 7 Habits of Highly Effective People*. Simon & Schuster UK Ltd Text drawn from Part One, Page 34
Page 27	3. Dilts, R. B. (2003) *From Coach to Awakener*. Meta Publications, US (The Neuro-Logical levels Model of NLP inspired by Gregory Bateson and developed by Robert Dilts in 1990)
Pages 33	4. Massey, Morris Dr. (1988) *What Works At Work*. Lakewood Publications.
Page35	5. Values of the political parties were sourced from their respective websites in 2014.
Page 134	6. Anthony Robbins, Coach & Motivational Speaker www.tonyrobbins.com

Acknowledgements

My heartfelt thanks and appreciation go to:

- my husband Mike and my parents for their love and support
- those who inspired me: Nancy Kline, Anthony Robbins, Mike Harris, Andy Harrington
- those who provided insights, research, content, ideas, proof-reading and editing assistance: Michael Beale, Carl Davies, Ali Stewart, Clint Adams, Arvind Devalia, Jackee Holder, Meg McAllister, Beryl West, Su Gerred, Trish Smith, Kim Horwood and my colleagues and the Pen and Ink Club
- my kind friends for their encouragement along the way, including: Deborah Polverino, Wendy Boast, Monica Potts, Peter Dixon, James Brown and the lovely Athena ladies
- all my amazing clients
- all my valued colleagues at UK Values Alliance, Human Values Foundation and Barrett Values Centre
- my wonderful team of Values Coaches

"Lindsay is a key member of the Steering Group of the UK Values Alliance and has contributed hugely to helping people live and work based on their values through this role and as one of the facilitators in our Wake Up To Values project within organisations. Lindsay brings to the UK Values Alliance wisdom and clear communication that greatly advances our vision of putting values at the heart of society. These same qualities make her book an invaluable guide. The easy to follow I-VALUE Coaching Framework in Part 2 is so well expressed and clearly presented that I am in no doubt that this will be a superb guide for so many people, not just coaches. Anyone interested in values and making a lasting difference to themselves and others will surely want to have this book by them constantly."

Maureen Watson, Co-Founder of the UK Values Alliance

"Lindsay's excellent book should be required reading not just for coaches but for anyone who wants to get their own life back on track. It explains clearly why values are so critically important in all aspects of our lives. It shows how we must become aware of our values in order to formulate the right goals, and how to live those values so we can achieve those goals. It also shows how ignoring those values inevitably brings us stress and unhappiness. This is an indispensable step-by-step guide from an experienced and successful practitioner, giving us everything we need to help us transform our own and others' lives."

Charles Fowler, Chairman of the Human Values Foundation

Author Biography

Lindsay West, the founder of Values Coach UK, is a respected and successful coach, trainer and speaker, and has trained an expert team of Values Coaches in her powerful values-based methodology.

Through her key role in the UK Values Alliance, Lindsay is pursuing her vision to promote the importance of values in society. She is driven by her passion to help others use their values to live happier and healthier lives.

In 'Coaching with Values', Lindsay shares her experience and proven techniques for putting values at the heart of coaching to make a lasting difference.

Printed in the United States
By Bookmasters